"The LOVEFiLM story offers interesting insights into the way modern businesses, and particularly those backed by venture capital, succeed. There are useful lessons for anyone looking to start or grow a business using this route. Simon Calver explains both the challenges and opportunities that VC funding raises. Calver is right to describe this as the classic modern business story."
Alex Mitchell, Head of Influencer Relations, IoD

"The LOVEFiLM story was a great read. It's honest, insightful and very entertaining. It shows most importantly the power of leadership to create an exceptional company. Frankly, everyone in the UK needs to read this book right now."
Julie Meyer, Managing Partner, ACE Fund

"I met Simon at the annual Real Business awards in 2009, and was delighted when he asked King of Shaves to become a founding member of The Consumer Forum – an association of SME's that put the customer first. The success of LOVEFiLM, and his leadership of this disrupting business, was entirely down to his 'putting customers first' – by giving them what they wanted, when they wanted it, always embracing the latest in cutting edge technology. Firstly by sending the latest film releases through the post, and now by it streaming on demand.

I've been lucky enough to spend personal quality time with him, and now you can learn how he helped LOVEFiLM grow so astonishingly, in a constantly changing digital environment. If you Lovefilm, and LoveCustomers, then you'll Love this book!"
Will King, Founder, King of Shaves

D1390533

"The LOVEFiLM story shows the importance of organizational agility, trust and the relentless focus of taking customers, stakeholders and employees with you on your journey. Above all it demonstrates the importance of understanding what you do and why you do it, and why it's important to have a business model that delivers for the customer and the business."
Jo Causon, CEO, Institute of Customer Service

"It took Simon's dedicated hard work bringing together a series of smaller businesses to make LOVEFiLM one of the true internet success stories. In Simon Calver's book, he shares his business philosophies that led LOVEFiLM to the successful takeover by Amazon. The book is not just a compelling narrative, but lessons that all businesses and entrepreneurs can benefit from."
Mark Florman, CEO, The British Private Equity and Venture Capital Association (BVCA)

"LOVEFiLM was a company Ella's Kitchen had looked up to as an example of being an innovator, the re-definer of its category and one that was truly customer centric. Simon was a CEO I had personally looked up to as someone who I thought defined leadership, rose to challenges and could think differently. I've had the privilege to see, almost from the inside, his style, vision, inclusiveness and clarity of thought which have inspired his team – and me too – whilst I have also benefited from the generosity of time and his willingness to share learnings with me. If I ever started again and were looking for a partner or non-executive mentor, I know who'd be top of my shortlist. Enough said."
Paul Lindley, Founder, Ella's Kitchen, www.ellaskitchen.co.uk

"Simon's considerable experience spans start-ups and multinationals, and his CV reads like an album of number one hits. You wouldn't know it to meet him though, he's ego and buzzword-free, offering straightforward insights based on nearly three decades building, fixing and growing great companies."
Richard Moross, Founder and CEO, moo.com

SUCCESS THE LOVEFiLM WAY

How to Grow a Fast Growth Business in Fast Changing Times

Simon Calver

CAPSTONE

Registered office

Capstone Publishing Ltd (A Wiley Company), John Wiley and Sons Ltd, The Atrium, Southern Gate, Chichester, West Sussex, PO19 8SQ, United Kingdom

For details of our global editorial offices, for customer services and for information about how to apply for permission to reuse the copyright material in this book please see our website at www.wiley.com.

Wiley publishes in a variety of print and electronic formats and by print-on-demand. Some material included with standard print versions of this book may not be included in e-books or in print-on-demand. If this book refers to media such as a CD or DVD that is not included in the version you purchased, you may download this material at http://booksupport.wiley.com. For more information about Wiley products, visit www.wiley.com.

Library of Congress Cataloging-in-Publication Data
Calver, Simon, 1964–
  Success the LOVEFiLM way : how to grow a fast growth business in fast changing times / Simon Calver.
    p. cm.
  Includes index.
  ISBN 978-0-857-08369-2 (pbk.)
  1. LOVEFiLM (Firm) 2. Video rental services–Great Britain. I. Title.
  HD9697.V544L683 2013
  384'.84–dc23   2012046225

A catalogue record for this book is available from the British Library.

Cover design: Parent Design Ltd

ISBN 978-0-857-08369-2 (paperback) ISBN 978-0-857-08385-2 (ebk)
ISBN 978-0-857-08382-1 (ebk)   ISBN 978-0-857-08383-8 (ebk)

Set in 10/13.5pt Sabon by Toppan Best-set Premedia Limited
Printed in Great Britain by TJ International Ltd, Padstow, Cornwall, UK

*To Monty James Calver and Nieve Elizabeth Calver
hoping you follow your entrepreneurial passions
and dreams.*

CONTENTS

INTRODUCTION

Thursday 20 January 2011 is hardly a day that set the history books alight. There weren't many major news stories that day. The year's big story, the popular uprising across North Africa and the Middle East that became known as the Arab Spring, had barely started. One news item that day, alongside the usual litany of unfortunate crimes and new political initiatives, was the opening of a shrine to Paul the Octopus in Germany. This marvellous marine creature had allegedly accurately predicted all the winners in the previous summer's football World Cup but passed away in October. I think it's safe to call it a slow news day.

But it was a big day for me and for the rest of the team at LOVEFiLM. It was also a pretty big day for everyone at Amazon, because it was the day we announced the deal in which Amazon took over the bit of LOVEFiLM it didn't already own. Amazon had been a major investor in the business, with a seat on the board, since 2008. In some ways it was no surprise to see Amazon purchase the rest of the stock. While some UK observers complained it was another example of a UK business being sold before it had chance to grow, the truth is that the earlier Amazon deal was one of the reasons the business had grown as much as it had since 2008. When the announcement was made to the staff, gathered at an all-staff meeting, they spontaneously broke into a cheer and a round of applause. That said a lot to me about this being the best possible news for LOVEFiLM. They were cheering because they knew it was the best deal. It was by no means inevitable. But even with a little sniping from some of the smaller investors, the deal went ahead and went smoothly.

Anyone lucky enough to have been part of a business that has grown as quickly as LOVEFiLM – particularly one that captured the public imagination the way we did – will tell you the journey is never straightforward. And it wouldn't have surprised me if there had been a final, unexpected twist in the tale. It is partly the unpredictability that makes leading a fast-growth business so interesting. And one of the reasons for this book is to attempt to translate those experiences into useful business lessons.

My involvement with LOVEFiLM may have culminated in the full glare of the media spotlight as we announced the Amazon sale, but it began in a much more low-key manner, over a coffee. There were no cameras and no journalists present. There wasn't even a press announcement about me joining. While some elements of the team, the company culture and its approach to customer service might still be the same, the company we sold to Amazon was mostly unrecognizable from the one I joined in 2005.

In the six years between those two dates my role as CEO was to lead the company through a near-constant process of change and evolution. Some of these changes were small and insignificant; the sort of thing that only those concerned ever get to know about. But others were huge. I led the company through a series of events that transformed it from a small, obscure, tech start-up into a well-loved household brand name. That transformation included mergers with rival firms and sensational marketing campaigns, as well as the defining deal with Amazon. Along the way we made some people very wealthy and brought lots of people lots of entertainment and happiness. It's always nice to enjoy your work, and as the CEO of a company, it is vital that you love the brand and company you lead. If you don't believe in what you're doing, it's difficult to take others with you and almost impossible to convince them to do things they might not want to in the interests of the wider company. The sale to Amazon was a defining moment in my personal LOVEFiLM and business experience. But as positive and exciting as doing that deal was, there was a part of me that was sad because I knew it would change LOVEFiLM forever.

The sale was the culmination of a journey that had begun almost a decade earlier, when a number of bright entrepreneurs and venture capital (VC) investors had the same idea at roughly the same time. Online video rental business Netflix was thriving in the US and taking that model and launching a version of it in the UK was an obvious win that was appealing to potential investors.

"In many ways the LOVEFiLM experience encapsulates the archetypal modern business story."

Companies such as ScreenSelect, Video Island, LOVEFiLM and Mov-iesbyMail stuck to the 1% innovation rule, in other words they were all basically variations on the successful Netflix business model. That meant there was a decent amount of evidence that the business would work. Each of these businesses that started and eventually merged to become LOVEFiLM International was slightly different. They each reflected the personalities of their founders. But the differences were marginal. Each was essentially an adaptation of the Netflix model for the UK. Although it is much smaller than the US, the UK nevertheless has a strong tradition in cinema and films. In the early 2000s, bricks and mortar DVD rental shops were still doing OK. But internet connections were speeding up and spreading across more of the UK and it was clear that the future for film distribution would be at least partly digital. While investors were still risking their money – and any start-up is always a risk – it was a calculated risk and one many were evidently prepared to take.

The business case clearly stacked up well enough for VC investors because a number got involved in backing these various start-ups. This involvement of multiple VCs became a defining characteristic of the business. In hindsight it was both a bonus and a drawback. It meant that when we eventually brought all the firms together under the LOVEFiLM brand, there were several VCs at the board table. While this gave us plenty of access to the brains, the support and the cash we needed to grow the business, it also meant that the pressure to secure an exit was significant. There was no question that people were at the board table to make sure they got the best possible return on their investment (both intellectual and financial), after all, this is the job they do for their investors.

In many ways the LOVEFiLM experience and the journey we went on as a team, encapsulates the archetypal modern business story. It involves fast-moving technology, VC investment from the start and the involvement of one of the biggest beasts in the modern technology market. In just under a decade we took a business from a series of start-ups, through mergers to a partial sale, through a period of rapid growth and then on to a full sale to a major global corporation. Along the way we experienced everything: a dramatic fire at our distribution centre, referrals and investigations by the Office of Fair Trading (OFT), rifts and fallouts between investors and management and takeover discussions with some of the biggest media and online businesses in the world. We didn't sit still for a minute and no two years were the same. And the Amazon ownership means LOVEFiLM has ended up as an essential part of one of the largest online businesses in the world.

My intention in this book is to tell this business tale. I believe the lessons it offers are powerful and general enough for it to act as a kind of extended case study. If you're a film buff, there should be something in this for you. But if you are interested in business, leadership and management, then I hope the lessons here will prove valuable. Most are drawn from my time in charge of LOVEFiLM, but some come from my earlier career experiences.

This is not intended as an autobiography. Instead, I prefer to think of it as the biography of a business philosophy. For a start, I wouldn't presume that anyone outside a very small circle – including my young son and new daughter whose reading is not yet that advanced – would have any interest in reading about my life. But in the course of a career that includes having worked at a senior level at several large multinationals, and, more importantly, having taken LOVEFiLM from start-up to sale, I have had some interesting business experiences. In particular the rules and processes, tips and tricks that have helped me through my career to date are worth passing on.

Of course that means talking a bit about the people and events that have shaped that philosophy. I have experienced life in vast multinationals and tiny start-ups as well as pretty much everything in between. This range of experiences has led me to form a philosophy for business that transcends the traditional barriers of organization size. I believe there are plenty of lessons that those in very large organizations can learn from those in the smallest companies and the same the other way round. Working for both types of business unfortunately isn't that common, but it makes for an exciting career for anybody.

My approach to business life – what might more grandly be called my business philosophy – has developed over many years and from a wide range of experiences. People prefer to digest the world by compartmentalizing it. But I think there are interesting insights to be gained from having been successful in both large multinationals and small start-ups.

Who decided that those working in small firms can't employ some big company thinking around issues such as data and performance management and measurement? While I know from experience that many large companies would love to behave more innovatively and entrepreneurially, making decisions more quickly and responding more rapidly to changing market conditions. I have worked for and led restructuring projects for some of the world's largest companies and I have turned around and grown very small, entrepreneurial businesses. While the circumstances and challenges each organization faced meant I learnt something different each time, I applied a common language and consistent approach to them all. It is this approach I hope to expand on and explain in this book. As well as telling the LOVEFiLM story along the way.

This book is split into three parts. The first tells the story of my early experiences and career and explains how I came to get the LOVEFiLM gig. The second tells my version of the LOVEFiLM story, with each chapter covering a year of our incredible journey. In this section for each chapter I have picked a classic film that seems to best sum up the events of that year. The final part of the book explores some of the lessons learnt along the way.

I hope there are plenty of valuable, practical lessons here for you to take away, whether you currently work in a large multinational organization or are running a local shop, which incidentally is where our story begins . . .

PART ONE

PRE-PRODUCTION

CHAPTER 1
OPEN ALL HOURS

The summer of 1976 was unforgettable. It was long, hot and dry. Drought stalked the British countryside, drying up streams and turning this green and pleasant land brown. But what I remember most from that summer is long afternoons lugging sacks of potatoes. Along with my two older brothers, I was working at my father's supermarket in Gloucester. My father was a firm believer in us getting stuck in. "If you can't carry a sack of potatoes, you're no use to me," he'd tell us. So we turned things like carrying potatoes into a contest and made it fun. Sometimes, however dull or mundane a job, you have to get stuck in and get it done. No one should ever think they are above doing those hard, menial jobs.

A PHILOSOPHY FOR BUSINESS

I can date the development of my business philosophy back this far. Certainly business has been a central part of my life from early on. Both parents ran their own businesses – and still do today – and many early memories are of helping my father in Calver's, a two-store chain of medium-sized local supermarkets in Gloucester. My grandfather started the business after WWII, and by the time I appeared Dad was running one branch and my uncle looked after the other. My mum is also entrepreneurial and when I was young she launched a hairdressing salon not far from our junior school.

"I spent my formative years watching customers, learning how they behaved, and dealing with them myself. It was a great early learning in merchandising, how to handle customers and how to run a business."

So business was a regular topic of conversation around the house when I was growing up (as were rugby and girls). The dinner table was often lit up with talk of a new idea or a new business venture. While it's impossible to know what makes entrepreneurs do what they do, my early years were a series of business lessons that made it inevitable that at some point my career would take an entrepreneurial twist. Interestingly both my brothers have also ended up running their own businesses.

Whatever I did was also likely to be customer facing. After all, I spent my formative years on the shop floor watching customers and learning how they behaved, how my father and his staff dealt with them and dealing with them myself. It was a great early learning in merchandising, how to handle customers and how to run a business. I learnt about stock management and things like how to manage the mark-up on fruit and veg and how it all generated profit. I remember watching my father work his magic with customers, offering "just a bit over" at the butcher's counter with a beaming smile everybody loved. The experience in-store stacking brands on the shelves was definitely one of the reasons why later on I ended up working in marketing and branding roles at a brand and product powerhouse like Unilever. I had no choice. Retail was in my DNA.

I also used to go with Dad when he took the cash to the bank, counting it out in the back of the car. That taught me the most powerful lesson there is in business: the importance of cash and cash flow. We probably took it for granted as the supermarkets flourished, but its importance hasn't diminished one bit. In fact, in this age of austerity, cash is arguably more important than ever.

The lesson on the importance of cash was one we chose to ignore when we took the decision at LOVEFiLM to spend a large chunk of the money we had in the bank to launch our first major TV advertising campaign. It was a calculated gamble. But I'm getting ahead of myself.

The first entrepreneur that I was aware of, even if he never described himself as such and died before I was born, was my grandfather. He worked for Lipton and was involved in food distribution during the war. It has never been discussed, but I suspect that meant sailing close to the line where "entrepreneurial" met the legally blurry post-war, ration-inspired black market. By all accounts he was a strong and forceful character. He was also partner in two cafes in Gloucester; funnily enough they were the only two in

Gloucester able to cook their chips in lard rather than the inferior rationed ground nut oil. They used to have queues outside them every night. This was how he made the money that funded the supermarkets.

WHAT'S THE POINT OF EDUCATION?

After the war he founded Calver's in Gloucester and later pulled my father out of further education to bring him into the business. This still irks my father today as his brother, my Uncle John, went on to get a scholarship to Oxford. With my other uncle, Dad took over as shop managers and co-owners of the business when my grand-father died.

The Art of a Good Gloucester Team

In Gloucester rugby is a religion not a sport, and as three boys we had no choice but to start playing at six or seven. We all learnt a lot about teamwork from rugby. To my mind rugby is one of the ultimate team sports. Anyone in business can learn from it. It's remained a passion of mine – and I am lucky enough today to have debentures at Twickenham. The key thing about a good rugby team is that you need individuals, each with their specialist positional skills, to combine well together to build a team. Props need to be props, technically good at scrummaging and lifting, flyhalves need to be flyhalves, quick and decisive, but both have to work together on the pitch, even if they don't drink together in the bar. This is a powerful analogy for the modern workplace where individual specialists are just as dependent on each other to produce a winning organization.

INNOVATE OR DIE

My father's shop was my defining experience growing up, at least until my parents split up. For all that my dad worked all hours; he also showed me the importance of taking time out. Sometimes when he was tired after a hard game of rugby, he'd lay out the toilet rolls upstairs in the storeroom and make them into the perfect bed. Then again, his nickname growing up was "kipper", because he had the ability to sleep anywhere.

Initially the businesses did well and both shops flourished. But it was a transitional time for shopping in this country and with the arrival of larger, less personalized supermarkets it was tough time to be running small, local stores. But we had a good life and both the shops were at the heart of their local communities. In some ways the success of the business was one reason it got into trouble. We didn't innovate in order to compete when Tesco came to town. Because we were comfortable we did nothing about it. But as those major supermarkets – and Tesco especially, which at that time under Jack Cohen was thriving as a "pile it high, sell it cheap" operation – moved into town, we couldn't compete on price. Customers started to drift off, one by one. I would go round to friends' houses and their mums would apologize for not being able to shop with us anymore.

Over time it got harder just to survive. In the end, the shops were sold and converted into Post Offices, which is what they still are today. Ironically you could say the same thing is now happening to Post Offices. But this was a bitterly painful early experience, seeing customers and friends walking away from the business, and it was, of course, discussed at home. It's always difficult to change when you are doing well, but if you do it then it is more effective and long lasting. If you leave it too late it becomes about survival and often you don't have time or resources to get it right. You always need to be moving forward, because it is onwards or out in most markets today.

NATURE, NURTURE OR A BIT OF BOTH?

Although I was more involved in my father's shop than my mother's hair salon, she was also a strong influence on me. I would go there and learn how a service-based business worked.

"The environment we grew up in has made us driven and entrepreneurial and instilled a belief that we can succeed with a bit of luck, a lot of hard work and a warm smile."

After they separated, Mum got a job in the salons on world cruises and then managed those salons, eventually settling in Sydney with people she met on-board. When she came back to the UK some years later she still had the drive to create a business and set up a beauty training school in Cardiff that was so successful she was shortlisted for Welsh businesswoman of the year.

In some ways she had more entrepreneurial drive and ambition than Dad. She now lives in Cyprus and has a lovely house in the hills where she runs tranquility retreats. She's always been a real self-starter, where my father has always been a server of people. He loves to have his own business so that he can be the host and offer great service. That was characteristic of his approach to the shops and other businesses he has run, including a sandwich bar. But my mother, while she loves to offer that good service, and has plenty of emotional intelligence, is more driven and ambitious. That combination was in our DNA from the start. So it was somehow inevitable that all three of their boys would run their own businesses. The environment we grew up in, perhaps combined with something in our DNA, has made us driven and entrepreneurial and instilled a belief that we can succeed with a bit of luck, a lot of hard work and a warm smile.

It's interesting that all three sons were initially drawn towards large corporations or institutions, rather than starting our own businesses straight away. After university I went to Unilever, then on to several other large companies; my middle brother Paul worked for British Aerospace; while Mark – the eldest – went into the police. Without getting too dramatic about it, I think that might have to do with our parents splitting up. It shattered our close family unit. My mother went onto the cruise ships, while my father moved to Devon and opened a smaller shop. Those large institutions became our families. Certainly I was more risk averse and more concerned with fitting in. I enjoyed the camaraderie and support structure of large organizations at that time.

LESSONS IN LIFE

Being 14 and having my mother disappear across to the other side of the world was tough, but it taught me resilience and independence. Initially, my father, brothers and I carried on living together. It was a very male-centric household.

After two years I was the one making sure the bills were paid. I took on that kind of responsibility. It made me grow up a lot quicker than other kids. I don't regret it, but it changed me. In a way, I think that early self-reliance is another reason I am ambitious and striving. When you experience something like that it affects your self-esteem.

People often confuse confidence and self-esteem, but there is a difference. It's a combination of high confidence and high self-esteem that can lead to arrogance; I have seen this in a number of people I have worked with. But the mixture of high confidence and low self-esteem I had at that time is perfect for entrepreneurs. It means I had the need and desire to drive myself on and prove things to myself, and the world. But I also had the confidence to carry it off. I believe that balance of high confidence and low self-esteem is the perfect formula for entrepreneurs.

THE THIRD GREAT UNIVERSITY

After school I went to the University of Hull. Blackadder famously claimed it as "the third of the great universities along with Oxford and Cambridge". He may have been trying to catch out a potential

German spy, but I'll settle for that. I was well prepared for life at university, because I had been looking after myself for a while. I knew how to cook and how to handle budgets.

But without my father's shop, I needed a new way to make money. Despite business ideas and ventures being talked about so much while I was growing up, I was never the classic schoolboy entrepreneur. I never hatched plans or businesses myself as a youngster, perhaps because I was too busy working in the shop. But at university I started to sell holiday vouchers to companies so they could offer them as incentives to customers or staff. I'll never forget that soft, southern boy knocking on the doors of businesses in Hull explaining what I was offering and asking if they would be interested in buying some. It was straight door-to-door selling and I could do it because of my self-confidence. I had always enjoyed acting and public speaking at school and that helped me selling. I had a second-hand grey suit but the only pair of shoes I had were brown. So I bought some grey paint-on die to make the shoes match the suit. At the end of two days walking round the industrial estates of Hull, my feet were blistered and the paint was peeling off my shoes. I must have looked a state, but I was still able to sell.

VARIETY OF INTERESTS

I got very involved in the university and became president of the Athletic Union, which meant running the sports for the university and managing a large budget. It was a lot of power for a student. I ran a team of six students and one permanent secretary. I even had my own office, which is more than I had at LOVEFiLM and more than I have now.

It was my first management role, and it was hard to fit in with full-time studying. But that role at the union was equally as important as studying, because it's the sort of thing that prospective employers look for when recruiting. I guess it helped to make me a more interesting and attractive candidate. I have always made the most of the opportunities presented to me and I like to try as many different things as possible. Unless you are going to be really good at one thing and you know what it is, the more things you expose yourself to the better. You never know where your strengths are going to be. And you meet more interesting people along the way and learn from them.

At the Athletic Union I sat on university council meetings. At the time the head librarian was the poet laureate Philip Larkin. Getting to know and work with people like that was all part of the experience. In fact he used to fall asleep in nearly every meeting, no doubt subconsciously composing his next great poem. But for all his calm exterior he used to terrorize people in the library with a withering look over his dark-rimmed glasses, quelling any noise or general student fun instantly. It was a great experience to meet these people.

THE WORLD OF WORK CALLS

When Unilever came up, as a typical student I left applying to the last minute and filled in the application very quickly. Fortunately, the first interview went well and they invited me to London to the grandeur of the Waldorf Hotel for the second interview. At this throwback to the days of the Empire, there were seven Oxbridge candidates and me. I held my own and I got into the Unilever Companies Management Development Scheme (UCMDS), the graduate programme. It used to take around 50 people a year and in the first year you spent a month in every function of the business. It was the best possible start in business.

The Early Lessons

1. **Don't underestimate the importance of understanding numbers** and getting to know the metrics behind a business when you are young.
2. **Get early experience of managing people.** I did that through things like the Athletic Union, being house captain, directing plays and captaining the rugby team.
3. **Learn to appreciate the importance of cash.** The most powerful lesson in business is the importance of cash. Its importance hasn't diminished one bit.
4. **Seek out some customer service experience early on** and learn all about what excellent customer service looks like. Working in the supermarket taught me about customer service and about the importance of milestones to help you get what you want to achieve.
5. **Understand the implications of everything you do.** I also managed my father's shop in the summer and I always wanted to beat his revenues and takings. I sometimes dented his gross margin percentage, but I beat his revenue target every time.
6. **If you don't innovate, competitors will steal customers.** My Dad's shops lost out to the major supermarkets. It's difficult to change when you are doing well, but doing it then is more effective. Leave it too late and you don't have time to get it right.
7. **Try as many different things as possible while you can.** Unless you are going to be really good at one thing, the more you expose yourself to new things the better. You never know where your strengths lie. And you will meet more interesting people along the way.

CHAPTER 2
LEARNING THE MULTINATIONAL WAY

At 9am on 5 September 1985 my career started. It was clearly not my first day's work as I had been working most of my life at my father's shop. But this was something new. I had only worked for small companies before. Unilever was my first experience of a large organization. And as first impressions of the world of work go, it was pretty good. In fact, I loved it.

I joined the Unilever Companies Management Development Scheme (UCMDS), starting at Lever Brothers, the detergent and cleaning company. It was like being part of a fantastic family. Twenty other graduates joined at the same time and we all got on well. Some of them remain my closest friends today. These first few years of work were really a continuation of university, with this integrated learning programme that involved us working together on different projects in different parts of the business. It was like being at university but with a salary. Even better was that we got paid expenses when we travelled. I thought I had died and gone to heaven. I couldn't believe work could be so much fun. Ever since then I have tried to make sure that people who work for me have some enjoyment in their work.

I was surrounded by scarily bright, smart, creative people and every year or so they put us on a business education programme with different people from other Unilever companies such as Birds Eye, Wall's, Elida Gibbs, Brooke Bond or Mattesons. Through this I learnt accountancy and marketing and the important general lessons you need to know to be able to run a business. It was great training and it's no surprise that many of the people who went through that scheme have gone on to run some of the world's most prestigious companies.

The people from that programme have gone on to an astonishingly wide range of roles. They include Benet Slay, now managing director of Carlsberg UK, Matt Kingdon, chairman and founder of innovation consultancy What If!, and TV comedian, actor and star of *Mock the Week* and the *Now Show*, Hugh Dennis.

The benefit of such a generalist training is that later in your career when you reach board-level positions, and you are expected to know how companies run, you can draw on a range of experience and knowledge. Too often people can reach the boardroom without a clue about what happens in business outside of their specialist area. This scheme meant we began to understand the finance function as well as marketing or sales or distribution. Everyone on the UCMDS spent a month in every function of the business and it gave us an excellent start and insight into the whole business. It equipped us with a sense of how each unit within the business worked, their interdependencies and it helped us build up a picture of how the whole company ran.

The Lever Bros head office was in Kingston, but they also had a factory in Port Sunlight, on the Wirral, and another in Warrington. Port Sunlight was the original Lever Bros factory. The business was founded by one of those great Victorian philanthropist industrialists, William Hesketh Lever. His idea of business as a force for good wasn't very fashionable in the UK in the 1980s when I worked there, but that philosophy stayed with me and it's good to see it at the forefront of business today.

William Hesketh Lever

William Hesketh Lever was one of the great Victorian philanthropists. Very much a man of his time, he believed in paternalism and looking after all aspects of his workers' lives. Along with the likes of Joseph Rowntree and the Midland's Quakers at Cadbury (who built Bournville, which is still regarded as one of the nicest places in the UK to live) Lever provided his employees with housing and made sure they were well catered for. The original Port Sunlight village is now a museum. Many of Lever's paternalistic ideas are regarded as old-fashioned and overbearing now. But there is still something positive to take from the central idea

(Continued)

and advertising, not because I was interested in the numbers. When I was younger I used to watch the advertising as much as the TV programmes and I used to help my Dad with making the rudimentary advertising posters for his shop with a block-print set.

After my first year at Lever Brothers I spent some time on washing up liquids, such as Squezy and Sunlight, and then I worked down in head office in National Accounts. That was a major leap for me. I got the role partly because of my background and the natural affinity I had for brands and retail after years working in the supermarket. In those days most people at National Accounts were older and longer in the tooth and had all worked their way up through the sales force to get to the central office.

I was one of the first young guns from marketing to make it into National Accounts and they let me know it, but I was determined to learn as much as possible. Because of my enthusiasm and store experience I managed to secure a placement at Tesco and *"A new customer* went off to the head office in Hertfordshire to learn *proposition has* how the different parts of that business worked. *to offer a win for* That was an excellent experience. Tesco had been *the business, a* instrumental in the demise of the Calver's supermar- *win for the* kets in Gloucester, and it was fascinating to see the *customer and a* business close up. That was just as Tesco was trans- *win for whoever* forming, under Ian (now Lord) MacLaurin, from the *is involved in* "pile-it-high, sell-it-cheap" operation it had been to *distributing it."* a more sophisticated, marketing-led outfit.

One insight during this time was the need to think through brand and customer propositions whenever you are innovating or developing new products. I was part of a team that launched a brand called Wisk Automatic. Ultimately it became the forerunner to the first Persil Automatic liquid, and that created an entirely new sector. It was exciting to be working on these products because it was a market sector where real innovation was happening. Wisk was developed because we wanted to see how the liquid product worked with consumers and how usage developed and so on, but we didn't want to experiment with the Persil megabrand in case the early results were negative and the feedback damaged the main brand.

During this time I really got to understand that any product or customer proposition has to offer a win for everybody. It has to offer a win for the business, a win for the customer and a win for whoever is involved in distributing it. With these new laundry washing liquids it was clear because while the customers benefited from the ease of dispensing as well as the perceived benefits of greater softness, it was also good for the business because people typically used more product per wash so the revenue per wash was higher. But it was also good for the retailers, because the new products grew the total market revenues, due to the higher cost per wash that meant they sold more through their tills. All parties benefited from the product, which is why the whole sector thrived.

Later on, at Pepsi I was in charge of the launch of Pepsi Max, which was another great example of a new product that achieved something for all parties. If you can find something that is good for the customer, the business and the channel selling it, you will be on to a winner. If there is nothing in it for one of those three, whether the trade, the consumer or the business, you are significantly less likely to succeed.

Win, Win, Win

Anyone thinking of launching a new product or service, whether in a new start-up or within a large organization, needs to consider what benefits they are offering to all stakeholders. It's fine to be customer-focused but you have to make sure that there is something positive in it for your suppliers or the distributors. At the other extreme there have been plenty of examples of new technologies that have not been about improving the customer experience;

(Continued)

they were just technology for technology's sake. Amstrad's combined home email device and phone, for example, just didn't take off because the perceived customer benefit wasn't great enough. It didn't do enough to resolve a customer pain point. Ideally a new product will mean a change that enables your business to be more successful, the customer to have a better experience *and* the channel or distributor base to benefit. If all three aren't getting something from it, it is less likely to succeed. All three are needed. If there's nothing for the customer, they won't bother to switch and if there is nothing in it for the channel they'll ask exactly the same question – why bother? And frankly, if there's nothing in it for you and your company, then just don't do it in the first place.

Unilever was a great institution then and it remains so today. But it dawned on me that there is only so much that was going to change and I could see ahead and see that I would be doing more of the same sort of work as long as I stayed there. At this time my head was also turned as I was headhunted by an interesting bunch of people, who had all worked for fast-moving consumer goods (FMCG) companies such as Mars, P&G or Unilever. They were working for a marketing strategy group within accountancy and consultancy firm Deloitte under a partner named Frank Milton. Frank was a smart, lovely guy who had pulled together this sharp bunch of marketing minds.

This was at the time that the old accountancy firms were taking on non-audit consultancy work. What was then known as Deloitte, Haskins and Sells had about 500 people. I was based in an office near the Old Bailey, my first job in the big City. It was great, I used to look out of the window and watch all the amazing things going on. I remember hanging out of the window seeing the Guildford Four being freed. It made for some interesting distractions from analyzing computer data.

My new role was all about data and getting right into the guts of an organization by looking at its information. This is where I really began to understand the power and importance of data and turning that data into valuable information. One mistake that some business people make is they get cut off from the essential metrics because their job becomes "bigger than that". It's a mistake because there's no better way to really understand a business than to look at the important metrics, better still if you can do that on a very regular, preferably daily, basis. Even as you get more senior, retaining the ability and desire to dive down and understand the key data is an essential one.

"The essential question for someone launching a new venture or taking over an existing one is to ask what data you need to run that business."

Anyone who leads a large multinational organization needs an amazing ability to understand data. I have been lucky enough to sit down with people like Michael Dell (founder of Dell) and Jeff Bezos (founder of Amazon) and something they share is this uncanny knack of being able to pick out a single number from a page full of figures and say, "that number doesn't work with that one and this doesn't add up". You just sit there embarrassed, thinking, "why didn't I see that?"

But the essential question for someone launching a new venture or taking over an existing one is to ask what data you need to run that business. Then you need to think about the frequency you need it and how you will manage it once you get it. And also how you can make sure you get the accuracy in it you need.

One of the most frustrating things for any leader or manager is when someone comes along and says they don't agree with the data or that the data is wrong. My view has always been to say that if the information is important for you in your job, then you need to take control of fixing data accuracy so you can believe it. It's imperative you have faith in the data so that you can take action and make decisions based on it. I have had experienced people turn up to a regular meeting every week telling me they don't believe the numbers. Even worse is the situation where the data only seems to be wrong when things are going wrong. If sales are down, the data's bad and if they are up we seem to have great data.

At Deloitte, with my numeracy training, computing knowledge and marketing experience I helped build a tool to do detailed analysis and econometric modelling of all the component parts of a marketing mix to try to understand how it worked. We used "Box Jenkins" statistical techniques to isolate some of the mix effects for a company and sold that to businesses to help them understand how their marketing was actually working.

I went around the country talking about it and selling the idea of why it mattered to understand how a company's marketing plans were working, as well as selling our specific service. We built up a nice little practice around econometric and marketing modelling, again looking at the metrics and understanding how businesses worked and why. It was a powerful and useful tool.

We tried to bring some harder statistics and modelling to the sector. We had a real hardcore statistician called Kerry who did all the data modelling and I was her "fluffy" marketing counterpart who knew the numbers. It was good for me because I was quite young and I had a product that I could go out and sell that challenged me. Rather than just be a consultant and sit in a room, I went out speaking to businesses about the importance of understanding marketing data and how to do it. I was 26 and was out selling consultancy and speaking at marketing events and I loved it. It met a need I've always had to be performing.

I was enjoying that but the firm got caught up in the huge consolidation that happened in the professional services sector and we merged with Coopers to form Coopers Deloitte (which later merged with Price Waterhouse to form PwC). Someone else took the Deloitte name. But the nature of the work we did changed after the merger. I became a more traditional management consultant working on very big projects. I was a small cog in a very large wheel.

One of those big projects taught me a particularly hard lesson. I was asked to run numbers and act as consultant on a job for an insurance company in Liverpool, pulling together all its independent financial advisors (IFAs), doing detailed analysis of revenue by advisor, by district, and by all sorts of other metrics. We were expected to offer a plan for restructuring the business based on that analysis. And I was asked in to do the restructuring and the reorganization.

At 27, I had to sit in a room with about 250 IFAs telling them they were going to be split into two groups. One group was going to keep their jobs, while the other group was going to be let go. I had to explain the process we would follow and how it would work. Then I had to do individual briefings with each of them explaining the process. You learn some harsh lessons when you sit in front of people twice your age and say, "you haven't got a job", especially in the late 1980s and early 1990s. You have to learn how to do it with empathy and how to respect individuals. It was a steep learning curve and to this day I never agreed that the company got external consultants to do its dirty work rather than do it itself.

The worst part of it was that about six months later I left the consultancy to join Pepsi. Before starting the new job, I took some time off and went travelling in South East Asia. I was in Bali at a place called Tannalot. It's a magical place where people go to watch the sun set behind a Hindu shrine. It is one of the most beautiful places in the world. As we were walking up to sit down to enjoy the sunset, I noticed some slightly older couples sitting talking to each other. One was telling the others how he used to work as an IFA for an insurance company and how they had got in consultants to get rid of half of them. This former employee was spending some of his redundancy money on the holiday of a lifetime. I was sat about 10 yards away from him and needless to say it took the gloss off the beauty of the sunset.

I left Coopers as the company became focused on very large jobs and I enjoyed client focus rather than working with big internal teams.

Through an ex-Unilever friend called Benet Slay, then at Pepsi (and now MD of Carlsberg UK), an opportunity arose to work at Pepsi launching Pepsi Max and then taking over marketing at PepsiCola UK. I took it and joined as UK marketing manager for Diet Pepsi and Pepsi Max.

They had been working on this secret new diet drink for ages, and while they were happy they had the product itself right, the marketing was problematic. The idea was to make the Pepsi Max brand stand out from Diet Pepsi with a more masculine brand positioning. But as hard as we tried to work with advertisers to get the creative right, we couldn't get it to work. We felt that the agencies didn't get it, and it was all a bit too worthy. Pepsi owned a US drinks brand called Mountain Dew that had this really exciting advertising with mountain bikers and skiers and all sorts of energetic stuff going on.

"Be prepared to borrow good stuff that already exists. As long as it's legal and you aren't infringing copyright."

In the end for Pepsi Max we just changed the can from Mountain Dew and cut and pasted the Pepsi Max can on frame by frame. It was a bit of a desperate last-minute measure to get us to launch. In the end we created the *Live Life to the Max* campaign and the first ad in particular turned into one of the most successful cola launch ads ever in the UK. And we'd borrowed the whole thing.

That taught me a valuable lesson in that there is no need to reinvent something if what you need is already there. Be prepared to borrow good stuff that already exists. As long as its legal and you aren't infringing copyright, don't be too precious.

The *Live Life to the Max* campaign was powerful and we won New Brand of the Year from *Marketing Week*. We also launched a great poster campaign that was "Full Cola Taste, Sugar Gets the Boot". It was a contrast ad similar to successful ads for *The Economist*. The inspiration was an internal ad drawn up for the team. That was "sh**load of taste, f**k all sugar". That was essentially the concept we were working to, we just needed someone to polish it and make it work. That simple, crude, statement summed up the brand tone and everything else followed from that.

When I arrived at Pepsi I didn't have a team. There was just me running the project. I had to work with the sales and marketing departments at Britvic, our franchise partner and joint venture. That helped in a funny way because it meant that I had to make sure that Pepsi Max was a win–win for lots of different areas of the business. In order to secure buy-in and support for the product I knew that other people had to see it as beneficial for them. When the marketing director left, and I became marketing director for the UK, I got my first taste of global marketing brand power.

Pepsi Max had gone well, but we soon found we weren't getting the standout on the supermarket shelf with our white Pepsi cans against Coke's red cans. We did lots of research and decided to change the colour of the can to blue. Although this was a global campaign, the UK was the first market to launch this new global product. The new product was initially called Pepsi Blue.

For the launch of Pepsi Blue we had this amazing worldwide PR machine and launched the whole thing in a hangar at Gatwick. We'd painted Concorde blue, if you could believe that, and (something the Tories have been trying to do for decades) we turned the *Daily Mirror* blue for the day. We had an amazing cast list including Cindy Crawford, Andre Agassi and Claudia Schiffer. I'll never forget one day presenting to some trade guests in the UK and I said I'd really like to get some of these celebrities in to meet them. I was called down in a lift and as the door opened there was Claudia Schiffer in a short leather skirt and fishnet stockings waiting to meet me. For once, I was lost for words.

As VP of the UK I had to stand out in front of the all the media and introduce everybody. It was another one of those performance moments I'll never forget. In that hangar I had to step out onto the podium and face a bank of 100 TV crews from all over the world. There were over 500 journalists and lights and cameras were everywhere. As I stepped out I thought, "oh my God, what have I done?" But it was such an adrenalin rush.

I'm glad I don't have to watch my stilted, high-pitched and stressed performance back now, but it was a real buzz at the time. And although we were slated in the UK press, because they said there was no substantive change in product, we kept on making a lot of noise and our sales increased. It was great fun, working on a huge brand with this enormous global budget. What I took from this time, meeting all these exciting people and doing these things on a global stage, was that it's essential you relax as much as you can, even under pressure, and enjoy things while they are happening. There is a lot of stress and pressure, but it is also very exciting. With hindsight I am sure the reason that the relaunch was slated so much was because one of the three wins wasn't there. For consumers, drinking out of a blue can rather than a white and blue can makes little difference. Unlike Pepsi Max, the product was the same and so the effect of the marketing "noise" was short lived.

Lessons from Big Firms

1. **Make sure work is fun.** As a leader, do whatever you can to make sure that people who work for you enjoy their work.
2. **Always look for simple solutions first.** If not everything can be fixed with a hammer, we can still overcomplicate problems.
3. **Understanding the numbers and metrics that are most important to measure** and knowing how you can effectively measure them is vitally important in any successful business.
4. **Make sure any new product or service benefits everyone involved.** Whether it's a new start-up or within a large organization, it has to offer benefits to all stakeholders.
5. **Know the data you need to run your business**, the ideal frequency you need it and how you will use it once you get it. And also how you can make sure you get the accuracy in it you need.
6. **Never reinvent something if what you need is already there.** Be prepared to borrow good stuff that already exists, as long as it's done legally.
7. **Take time to enjoy what you do and the experiences you are having.** It's essential that you relax as much as you can and enjoy things while they are happening.

CHAPTER 3
BECOMING A DELL BOY

There is an ongoing debate in the business community about whether people or strategy comes first. I got my first real insight into this question while working for Pepsi. In 1995 PepsiCo International lost about $500 m, on a turnover of £2 bn, and that was tough.

There were a lot of currency devaluations and write-downs that didn't help, but the structure of our international franchise business had evolved to become fundamentally flawed and was in need of a radical restructuring. After heading up marketing for the UK, I had gone off to be managing director in Ireland and to work with the Cantrell and Cochrane bottling franchisees there.

I was now called to New York, where the head office was based, and was asked to help create a new organizational structure for the world-wide franchise business. I was called in partly because I had been a management consultant, but I think it was mostly for the simple reason that I was responsible for one of the largest international franchise markets.

We were a small team of about a dozen people and we were given freedom to look at, and work through, the whole organization. Like most companies, PepsiCo's organizational structure had developed gradually. It had evolved over time and each different region had its own infrastructure, with its own marketing, sales, HR and finance functions. Although the world was increasingly global, these regions weren't talking to one another. They were all little fiefdoms, run by people who enjoyed being CEO or "El Presidente" of their own business and wanted to control their own units. The idea of this independence might have sprung from the theory on empowering strategic business units to make local decisions, sometimes referred to as functional business units. But although these had started off well they had developed into dysfunctional business units.

It added a lot of cost and overhead and meant there was a lot of fat across the business. And it was fat we couldn't afford to carry. Worse, there was hardly any sharing of best practice across the group.

As a team we split the work into two streams. One defined the work we needed to do as a global franchise business, while the other stream looked at the company-owned businesses. Having, at a high level, identified the critical work and business processes that needed to be done, we then went about focusing on how to track and measure this work to create the critical performance indicators that each part of the business was responsible for. Using this information we created the jobs needed to do the work effectively. Finally for each one of these roles we then built the job descriptions and highlighted the skills needed to be successful. That way we were able to define the right organizational structure and have the toolkit for selecting and training people in their new roles.

"Too often people starting a new venture get caught up in creating an organization to fit the whims and preferences of people they like to work with."

What was important was that we started with a blank canvas. We didn't think about the people, or what was already in place. We just defined all the jobs within the organization. Looking back now this was a powerful lesson for me. It's something all start-ups should think about. Too often people starting a new venture get caught up in this whole attitude of creating an organizational structure to fit the whims and preferences of people they like to work with. But having the right structure is critical for success. People have to understand who is responsible for what and who is doing what work and how they will be measured against that work.

"It is not enough just to employ brilliant people, you need to employ them in a brilliant structure, and you need them to be doing the right stuff."

It's not that structure is more important than staff, but you have to think about the two together from the start. And most start-ups think about the people above all else. But the right people in the wrong structure won't work and neither will the wrong people in the right structure. You need both to be right to get it right. The wrong people, doing the wrong things, is a major reason so many potentially good ideas fail to develop into successful businesses. It is not enough just to employ brilliant people, you need to employ them in a brilliant structure, and you need them to be doing the right stuff.

The Importance of Structure

The most important lesson from my time as a consultant and my work with PepsiCo was that even large global businesses need to get their structure right. When you make a change in structure and you put the right people in the right positions and measure their performance against the right objectives, you can see a transformation in results.

I used the same approach later at Dell and again at LOVE-FiLM. And there are lessons here that small companies can learn from large organizations. Even in a start-up I would spend time working out RAM – Roles, Accountability and Measures. You need to have success factors, and you have to make sure you appoint people against those factors. You have to make sure everyone is clear what's expected from the start. And as someone who has worked in a start-up, I understand that it is easier to say than do, especially when everyone is moving at 100 miles an hour.

Although you need this from the start, the time when this comes into its own is when you move from a start-up to a more mature structure. And believe me, when things go well, that can happen very quickly. If you have over 20 people in an organization, then spend time working out what their real roles are and where there is any overlap. And think about it earlier rather than later. Most people are surprised just how early in the life of a company you need to think about this stuff.

Within the space of six months the team redefined something like 35,000 jobs. In launching that new business structure we removed about $100m worth of cost and set the business on the right track, with the right metrics and the right clarity behind what was being done. We transformed the management and leadership of the organization and it became incredibly successful.

It was a great lesson for me and it was the first experience I had of markets such as China, India and Russia. What I discovered then and later in my role as VP for Sales Operations worldwide for PepsiCola is that wherever people are, and regardless of the cultural context they operate in, the basic motivators that drive all human behaviour, especially at work, are pretty consistent. I'd be in meetings in India or China and, even though I didn't understand the language the meeting was conducted in, it became clear that it was about the same things as I had experienced in other markets when the meetings were in English.

Not surprisingly, people want a clear role that is well understood and defined; they want to know they're adding to the big picture and they want the right training to do that job. And they want respect from their peers. Those basic human needs remain the same wherever you go. It is about trying to understand people's motivations. If you want to change an organization and have success in driving results you really need to try to think about how the organization is delivering against that, and you need to have the right culture and environment to make sure people understand.

But even though we'd built best practice global sales operations tools, we found a problem that many people find in large organizations, in that everyone thought they were the ones doing the best practice. The only way I got around this "not invented here syndrome" was to promise to roll out globally any initiative found to be better than current best practice. But it had to be tested, measured and proven. Fortunately, very few ever managed to prove us wrong.

A major lesson from this whole exercise was the importance of having total support and commitment from the top of the organization. At PepsiCo, I had to write and redefine my boss's job description. Wayne Mallioux was President of European Operations and I sat him down and talked him through how we were restructuring his role. That's not something you get to do very often in a large corporate structure. But if this sort of transformational project is going to have any chance of success, you have to have that support and endorsement from the very top. When you work in consultancy you often find that a great piece of work fails because it doesn't have support from the very top. Without that endorsement a lot of money is wasted.

At the end of that project I came back and redefined my role as VP of UK, including Ireland. I was working again for Wayne, the boss I had to brief on his role. Over time Wayne became a great mentor to me and he remains one of the best bosses I have ever had.

For the bottling business we launched a programme called Total Bottler Management. In some ways the approach there sums up my whole approach to people and strategy. It started with the question: What is the vision we are aiming to achieve? Then we looked at the key goals we needed to achieve to fulfil that vision and the milestones we needed to hit to know we were on target. Next we defined the specific strategic activities we needed to get involved in and the things we needed to prioritize to make sure it all worked. Finally we looked at the activities that would help achieve all of that.

"Start-ups can still aspire to the best bits of big company thinking in the same way that large corporates often aspire to be entrepreneurial."

This was our framework for strategy execution. People make strategy out to be very complex. But when it comes to it, all you need to think about is what you are trying to achieve, how you will get there and that you are sure you are focused on the right activities to do that.

All this may sound a little too safe and slow and big company to relate to a start-up. And in most cases it is too much. If you can do this stuff at the start, then great, but there is a time as a start-up when you don't have the resources to do analysis and get the perfect data. You often have to make decisions with imperfect data and you are usually flying by the seat of your pants and making calls on instinct. Undoubtedly that's the right thing to do in that situation but you need to know what you are not doing. To be deliberate about not having the time to take certain steps is different from not knowing you should ever take them. Start-ups can still aspire to the best bits of big company thinking in the same way that large corporates often aspire to be entrepreneurial. And even in the frenzy of a start-up, you should be able to take a step or two back before you make major decisions to ask whether you have the resources and cash to make it work. If you can do it, do it, but if you can't, know what you are not doing and as soon as you get the time and resource, start doing it.

By this time I was back to the US for PepsiCo to manage and restructure the global sales operation. I was in the US for three years just as the dotcom boom was happening. I had a degree in computer sciences and knew what was going on. I watched it all happen. And my entrepreneurial impulse was excited. I could see companies building themselves up and being sold for incredible valuations. Eventually I decided it was time to leave beverages and get involved in technology. But even though I made the leap to technology, I still wasn't quite brave enough to do something entrepreneurial, so I joined Dell rather than a pure start-up.

As it happens, in 2000, that was the right thing to do. I didn't know it at the time, but the tech bubble was about to burst and a lot of internet start-ups crashed, especially in the US where the bubble had been more pronounced. I joined Dell Computers, working alongside Paul Bell, the president of Europe, for three months to understand the business. Then I became VP and general manager of the home and small business division for the UK and Ireland. As this included businesses with up to 3,500 employees, it meant about 90% of all businesses. So for the first time I was selling into and trying to understand both start-ups and SMEs, which was really interesting and I learnt a lot about their businesses and how technology was helping them gain competitive advantage against the big boys.

By that time, Dell was a $20 bn business. I was responsible for a business worth $1.5 bn that employed 1,500 people. I was fortunate enough to work closely with Michael Dell on his trips to Ireland (where I was based) and got to learn a lot from him. He is a fantastic leader and it was impressive to watch this founder, leader and visionary and how he worked with his team and how – even though he was a relatively shy, techy person – his charisma, vision and passion for what he was doing really came through. He was less comfortable in front of large crowds compared to one-on-one meetings, but he had the energy and the vibrancy and the passion to pull a wide range of people along with him.

And the company was flying at that point. Success was measured in our growth. We originally targeted growth of three or four times what the market was doing overall. If the market grew 10%, we wanted to grow 30 or 40%. But after 2001 the world toughened up and the market changed as recession hit. Then we switched target and aimed for a market gap. If the market was flat we wanted a 30% gap to be maintained, so we wanted to grow at 30%. The point was that regardless of the circumstances we'd do whatever we had to do to get growth to about 30 to 40%. Achieving that growth target required me to get involved in an extraordinary level of detail. It was astonishing, but it showed me that there is no time the leader of a business can safely feel they are above getting involved in the day-to-day running of the business.

I used to have a daily "pulse" meeting at 11am where the heads of every bit of the business came in and told me what had happened the day before, what was working and what wasn't working. It was limited to 15 minutes and everyone stood up and it was all on one sheet of paper projected onto the wall. We would have a discussion and then go off and meet the next day. Sometimes it was high-fiving fantastic results, and giving a bottle of champagne to somebody, while other days it was about what we were doing wrong, why things weren't working and what we needed to do.

Those daily pulse meetings taught me the importance of establishing the rhythm of any business even as a start-up. I learnt to ask questions any leader should ask:

- What is the rhythm of your metrics or reporting?
- How often do you get reports on key data?
- When do you meet your main reports?

"A business can only be successful in the long term when there is total transparency to everyone within the organization."

For me it was about ensuring that people in my team and their reports understand the rhythm of reporting and frequency and structure of decision making.

Dell also taught me that maniacal focus on metrics. Michael Dell was always sending emails saying things like "Simon, your missing, wrong and damaged figure looks slightly high. Is there a reason, are you selling something wrong or is there a different reason?" I now see that the level of transparency of data, available to all levels, was essential to Dell's success at that time.

A business can only be successful in the long term when there is total transparency to everyone within the organization about its metrics. Everybody has to see everything. It's the best way to make everyone accountable. If you're all in it together, then you're all in it together. You need to share each other's metrics and if an area of the business isn't functioning well everyone needs to know because they might be able to find a way to make it better. But the markets Dell operated in were getting increasingly tough and the business had some tough choices to make. But I also personally think the people at the top made some bad decisions. It increased its focus on cost, which meant there was a loss of focus on customer service. I struggled as I can't work in an organization that doesn't always put the customer absolutely first.

This manifested itself as an acceleration of moving business to offshore call centres and although in the UK there has been a backlash against that now, at the time it became another cause of poor customer experience. Consumers in the UK weren't getting the service delivery they needed and the only people they could speak to about it were overseas and didn't understand the specific problems of UK consumers.

The other thing was that Dell had a strategy of not investing as much as competitors in new products or research and development. The strategy was focused on "time to volume", rather than "time to market". This meant it was focused on developing products it knew it could quickly sell lots of, rather than creating innovative new products. This can be a sound philosophy in some markets and was in Dell's case for many years. But in hindsight when time to market and innovations such as Apple's iPhone and iPad are driving your market, if you are too late in terms of getting to market, then you never get to volume because the market has already gone elsewhere. So in my mind you have to have a certain investment in product development and consumer research even if this is ahead of the curve. Dell's approach at the time was cost driven and there wasn't enough R&D activity.

But, similar to what I led at Pepsi, I did some major restructuring work at Dell and we turned the European consumer business around to being a profitable business as a result of those changes. We spent a lot of time understanding how sales were made and developed a model for the internet . . . as opposed to call centres. We enhanced the online product configuration process. In the interim people could go online and look at something and then call and order it. The idea was that the consumer decided and configured exactly what they wanted, or rather, exactly as the sales person wanted to sell it. We called this "internet-enabled sales" rather than pure online sales and what I learnt here formed the basic principles of how most multi-channel retailer strategy works today.

The other big learning I took was that Dell had a lot of focus on cash conversion (see box). Cash conversion is about how quickly you get cash in as opposed to how long it takes you to pay it out. Getting that balance right, so that you get paid upfront where possible, is critical to getting a positive cash flow. If cash is king, then a good business model with a positive cash conversion cycle is the real power behind the throne.

The Cash Preservation Society

Every small business owner understands the importance of cash. Some people in larger organizations even have to think about it, too. A positive cash flow can make or break a business, especially at a time when credit is harder than ever to come by. But not enough business people think about how their business model feeds into cash flow. This is where the cash conversion cycle comes into play. It is something I really learned at Dell and is essentially how quickly you get cash in as opposed to how long it takes you to pay it out. If the cash conversion cycle is positive, you gain cash as you grow. But if it's negative, you lose cash as you grow. Everyone at Dell understood that. It takes money from the consumer (so that is in the bank), then assembles the computer with parts that were ordered on 60- or 90-day terms. They were then sent to a shipping company on 45-day terms and, finally, they paid the people who assembled the computer at the end of the month. The company had a really positive 40-day cash conversion rate. In the very early days of LOVEFiLM getting the right cash conversion cycle right and ensuring that the business was making cash as it grew was essential. It meant I wasn't constantly going to investors seeking new finance as we grew. The subscription model is always a good way of having a positive cash conversion cycle, because people pay subscriptions upfront, before you buy DVDs or pay suppliers.

Dell eventually started to struggle as the after effects of the tech crash were felt. Then came 9/11, a recession followed and there was a major reorganization. Some people came over from the US to manage different parts of the business. I knew it would be a tough time to find a job, but I decided that the time was right for me to do something new and I agreed to take redundancy. That episode registered the importance of not getting caught out by corporate culture. I hoped to take a senior European position at Dell, but in the end they flew over an American to do the job and he wanted his own team. The message is that in large organizations you have just got to be careful of the culture and new people coming in, and often it's not personal, people just want different teams in. Nevertheless it can be very difficult for some people. I knew it was time for me to move on. I vowed never to work for a large US multinational again. With Amazon coming later in my business life, this was possibly my "Sir Steve Redgrave moment", who asked anybody who saw him near a boat again to shoot him after his fourth Olympic gold medal, before going on to win a fifth.

After Dell I went to run a small, interactive education company called RiverDeep. Run by experienced corporate bankers, it had just been through a management buyout. The story was that they were preparing the company for the next stage of growth and wanted someone to come and run it. I did some consulting with them and thought it was a great opportunity. It was a San Francisco-based company, although its corporate HQ was based in Ireland, which was how I knew them.

The initial idea was that I would spend one week a month in San Francisco. But that soon turned into three weeks in the month, when it became clear that this was much more of a turnaround than I had thought despite my due diligence the company was in a worse state than expected when I took over. It was a relatively small, $100 m company – that may be a size that many start-ups dream of, but it was small compared to Pepsi and Dell – and cash was critical. The finance director phoned me early on and said: "Simon, I'm not sure how we are going to pay the salaries this month" . . . that's when I began to realize what life is like for small businesses; it is often just about surviving.

RiverDeep formed as the result of a number of mergers of different companies, such as Edmark that was spun out of IBM and the Learning Company that demerged from Mattel. RiverDeep was an Irish company and was heavily into CD ROM, which by then was an aging technology. The critical issue was that although it was a $100 m business, it was losing a significant amount a year in the retail sector because the CD ROM market was imploding, retailers weren't putting CD ROMs on shelves anymore and all the returns being sent back or worse still discounted to nearly nothing were killing the business.

I looked in detail at the business, and this is a great example of how you should always try to cut up and dice a business in as many ways as possible. The analysis of the retail sector showed that if we set up a licence agreement and outsourced the retail business for a guaranteed return of a licence fee we could turn a significant loss of a year into a very healthy profit in just one deal. It transformed the business. On the back of that we were able to do a high-yield bond offering that restructured our debt, and we exited the original VCs who were still in the business, which allowed us to do some of the other things we wanted to do to grow the business, because it was on a stronger footing.

It goes back to doing that analysis of what a business does, asking whether all channels are equally profitable and looking at profitability by product line and by channel, and having identified that, making decisions, sticking to them and executing to that plan. It can transform the business as a result. I often hear of businesses that are inherently good businesses, where one part is losing lots of money and dragging the business down. You have to think about selling that division or licensing content or just trying something differently to turn it around. It gets back to the idea that sometimes it pays to use a little big company thinking in smaller organizations.

A lot of behaviour in small companies is a result of the way things have always been done or the way the founders liked to do things. That doesn't mean they are still the right things to do or that they are being done well. What small business owners rarely have is the luxury of time to stop and look at all aspects of the business to ask if things are working as well as they could. That is where non-executive directors or interested, active investors can help. The outsider's perspective can be hugely beneficial. It gets right back to making sure that you have the right basic plan in place and that the balance between strategy and people is right. Getting all that lined up is a lot more difficult to do than it is to say. But it is usually fun trying to get it right, whether the business is large or small.

Eventually commuting to San Francisco got to me. Having had a taste of running a small business, I went looking for something similar but based in London. I was having coffee in London at the Institute of Directors with an entrepreneurial investor friend, Saul Klein. He had launched an online video rental business in the UK called Video Island. He had talked to me about taking a role there a few years earlier, but it wasn't the right time for me. He explained how the business had come on and how they had since merged with another company called ScreenSelect and had major plans for expansion. He said they still hadn't found the right person to be CEO of the company and asked if I was interested. What an interesting skinny latte that turned out to be . . .

More Lessons from Big Firms

1. **Start with a structure and select the best people.**
Don't start a new venture with structure made to fit the
whims and preferences of people you like. You have to
think equally about the best structure and the best people
from the start.

2. **It is not enough just to employ brilliant people**, you
need to employ them in a brilliant structure, and you need
them to be doing the right stuff.

3. **The basic motivators that drive behaviour at work are
pretty consistent.** Wherever people are located, and
regardless of the cultural context they operate in, they want
the same things.

4. **Strategy is much simpler than some people make it
appear.** But when it comes to it, all you need to think
about is what you are trying to achieve, how you will get
there and that you are sure you are focused on the right
activities to do that.

5. **Start-ups should aspire to the best big company
thinking.** And in the same way, large corporates should
aspire to be more entrepreneurial.

6. **Transparency is key to success.** A business can only be
successful in the long term when there is total transparency
within the organization about metrics. Everybody has to see
everything. It's the best way to make everyone accountable.

7. **If cash is king, a positive cash conversion cycle is the
power behind the throne.** A good business model means
that every new customer brings in more revenue than they
cost the business.

CHAPTER 4

2003-4: THREE MEN AND A BABY

Why success has many fathers but failure is an orphan

Three Men and a Baby

Released: 1987

Director: Leonard Nimoy

Cast: Tom Selleck, Steve Guttenberg, Ted Danson

Synopsis: Three bachelors find themselves forced to take care of a baby left by one of the guys' girlfriends.

Awards: None

Trivia: As well as being directed by *Star Trek*'s Dr Spock, *Three Men and a Baby* was the highest-grossing movie of 1987 and remains the highest-grossing remake of a French film ($167,780,960) in North American box office history. Revenues for the film were further boosted by some none-too-subtle product placement when Pampers paid $50,000 for their brand of nappies to be used in the film.

"Victory has many fathers while defeat is an orphan" was President Kennedy's response to the Bay of Pigs fiasco. In business we rarely talk in terms of victory and defeat, and the consequences are rarely as serious as they were for JFK. But we do talk about success and failure and the JFK theory applies just the same. It's not difficult to find people keen to be associated with a success story, while naturally their CVs rarely benefit from being closely connected with a failure.

LOVEFiLM is an example of a success that has many parents. This is true both literally and metaphorically. Because of the nature of the early years of the business and the way that a number of different businesses operating broadly the same model came together, and the way that equity was raised by a number of those companies, there are a huge number of people who can honestly lay a claim to be involved in the early years of LOVEFiLM.

The choice of film for this year therefore reflects the start-up proposition at LOVEFiLM and other companies that formed with the same idea around the same time and subsequently merged to create LOVE-FiLM International. In fact there were three babies and nine men, or was it four babies and a football team? Either way, there is no shortage of people who can – and do – lay claim to being responsible for founding LOVEFiLM (see the Castlist box on page 59).

THE ONE PER CENT RULE

In simple terms what happened was a lot of entrepreneurial people and investors saw the same opportunity at the same time. For the most part, they saw what a company called Netflix was doing in the US and worked out that there was an opportunity to offer the same service in the UK. It is a classic example of the safest kind of innovation. Changing one aspect of an already proven business model (in this case moving the business from the US to the UK) is the sort of deal investors like. It's not as risky as something completely new and radical. It relies on existing technology that people understand and can see working and that makes it easier to examine and weigh up the business plan.

Where the Story Started

The Netflix story is a classic example of an entrepreneur solving his own problem. In 1997 founder and CEO Reed Hastings had rented *Apollo 13*, lost it and was facing a $40 fine. The recent arrival of DVDs into the industry made a mail-order rental business worth investigating (a fact tested by Hastings in the simplest way, by buying a bunch of DVDs and mailing them to himself). Initially nothing more than a "Blockbuster by post", in 1999 Hastings and co-founder Marc Randolph hit on the idea of adopting a monthly subscription fee, offering unlimited rentals and no late fees. In 2000 it devised a film recommendation system based on member ratings. Having raised £2 m seed capital at launch, an IPO in 2002 raised a further $80 m, despite having only 600,000 members at that time. By 2005 that had risen to 4.5 million users and membership now stands in excess of 20 million worldwide. It launched a streaming service in 2007.

In 2001, the internet/technology bubble burst. This caused a significant recession in the US. While the UK shivered, the economy kept growing and the entrepreneurial and investor communities started to look at ways of bringing some of the more successful US ideas over here. Several people spotted the opportunity to take the Netflix model and bring it to the UK. That meant that several entrepreneurs started businesses offering online DVD rentals at more or less the same moment. Each of these businesses was created in the image of its founders and funders and was therefore different to the others in approach, culture and structure. That made bringing several of these businesses together as one company (and getting several founders and investors around one board table) quite a challenge later on.

Family Tree of the Early Years

2002 Paul Gardner and Graham Bosher launch Online Rentals Limited (trading as DVDsOnTap).

Simon Franks CEO of Redbus and Anthony Ceravolo found Video Island and hire in Saul Klein as the CEO. Danny Rimer (Index Ventures) and George Coehlo (Benchmark Capital) become the main VCs in the business.

2003 William Reeve and Alex Chesterman, funded by Octopus Ventures and many business angels including Simon Murdoch, launch ScreenSelect. Arts Alliance Ventures – a family-owned private equity firm led by Thomas Hoegh – buys Online Rentals Ltd. DVDsOnTap is rebranded LOVEFiLM. At the same time ScreenSelect acquires In-Movies.

2004 ScreenSelect is acquired by Video Island to form a larger business with significant VC (now including Simon Cook's Cazenove Private Equity) and angel investors.

2005 The new Video Island acquires DVD 365, a Scottish DVD rental business. In August LOVEFiLM, with its new backers, acquires Boxman in Sweden and in September Video Island acquires Brafilm, the industry leaders in Sweden and Norway.

2006 LOVEFiLM and Video Island merge to form LOVEFiLM International; the new business acquires Digitarian, the leader in Denmark.

LET BATTLE COMMENCE

The stage was set for a viscous and fiercely contested competition between Video Island and LOVEFiLM. As I mentioned, each of the businesses that eventually made up LOVEFiLM International – LOVE-FiLM, ScreenSelect and Video Island – all showed the strengths of their founders. LOVEFiLM had the strongest brand and some exciting marketing, ScreenSelect had an excellent operating system and was very good at extracting the key data and metrics on the business, while

Video Island had strong financial backing and cash on the balance sheet. When they were eventually all pulled together, that combination of an excellent operating system, strong marketing and branding and a solid financial backing made for a compelling business.

Some of these businesses were better prepared for the challenge of scaling and coping with growth than others. When you run a membership rental business and it is small and you have 50 or even 500 members and a limited collection of DVDs, you can almost run it out of a suitcase under your bed. You are looking at a handful of DVDs coming in and out in a day. It's easy to manage. But it gets very complex very quickly. As soon as you have 5,000 or 50,000 members it is impossible to run this sort of business without very smart people doing very clever things with software and technology. Online DVD rental sounds like a simple enough business idea to launch, but it is extremely complex and hard to get right and scale. Very quickly you realize that if your customer experience is not spot on you will lose customers. The critical differentiator between many of these companies was not the ability to attract customers but invariably it was the ability to retain them or manage churn as we called it.

WHY BUSINESS IS ABOUT MORE THAN GOOD IDEAS

The algorithms you need to manage the business quickly become very complicated. You need to work out how you can best leverage your DVD base so that people get the right discs, you need to think how you will allocate discs to people when there is excess demand versus supply, and you need to know the right number of any disc for you to carry. It becomes very difficult and quite challenging to scale.

"A good idea on its own is not enough to succeed in business. To be successful you need the talented people to help implement it."

Whether it was by luck or judgement, the series of mergers that happened were very important in turning LOVEFiLM into a business more likely to succeed than fail. What strikes me looking at the major three players is that a good idea is not enough to succeed in business. To be successful you need the talented people to help implement it. In fact I would argue that in order to really succeed you need good talent doing the right work, i.e. which allows excellent execution; you need a board that is aligned with management and focused on a shared objective; and you need a healthy balance sheet (i.e. you need cash).

IT'S THE PEOPLE, STUPID

In the start-up businesses I have spent time with it seems too often people haven't thought enough about the people they are launching the new venture with. This is an area where start-ups would in my view benefit from some of the thinking and actions of larger organizations. When a group of friends start a business, it may be that you have to accept the skills of the people prepared to join you in the venture. But at the very least the start-up should think about who is missing and know what is not being done or not being done well enough. A large company would draw up an ideal candidate specification for every position. And in the same way start-ups should think about the key tasks and responsibilities of each post and the skills required to achieve those responsibilities, then see how that matches with the profiles of the people in the business.

What usually happens is that Greg does the accounts because he's better with numbers while John does the marketing because he did a summer as an intern at an agency. But excellent execution requires excellence in all areas and investors these days will be more likely to back a business that has the right people in place. The old adage about success being 5% inspiration and 95% perspiration has never been truer. Small businesses often make do and mend with the skills of the founders for too long. They leave it too late to go out and find new talent to drive the business forward. This is often because they don't think they can afford new staff. And bringing in new talent can be difficult and time consuming. But if you have the confidence and get it right it can make all the difference to the eventual success of the business. And done correctly it should bring increased revenue and should open up new sources of investment. Better still is the situation where investors also offer some of that talent and business wisdom themselves and that was definitely the case at LOVEFiLM.

Every business needs talent to make an idea work. Whether it's their own talent or that of the people they attract to the business after start-up. Talent certainly wasn't lacking in any of the businesses that came together as LOVEFiLM International.

The Castlist

The producers, directors and the star cast from LOVEFiLM's formative years

Alex Chesterman is regarded as one of the UK's leading internet entrepreneurs. He was co-founder of ScreenSelect, which merged with Video Island. He has since gone on to co-found successful property website Zoopla. He's also one of the best business development people I've ever worked with.

William Reeve was the other co-founder of ScreenSelect. He's a phenomenally bright guy and understands business metrics and how to get the right data and information out of a business like few other people. He's since gone on to work with numerous other entrepreneurs and investors. He is now COO at PaddyPower PLC.

Saul Klein is a legend in the technology investment community. Part of a family of investors, he was the CEO of Video Island and was the early driving force that got it established. He is now involved with a number of businesses, and set up the investment house Seedcamp.

Robin Klein is Saul's father and a force of nature. He was part of the original investment set-up.

Anthony Ceravolo was the first MD of Video Island and author of the first business plan.

(Continued)

Graham Bosher was the founder of DVDsOn Tap and the brains behind much of the technology. Graham left LOVEFiLM not long after the merger to form Graze, an incredibly successful, VC-backed, subscription food and snack business.

Simon Franks is the founder of Redbus, the content and entertainment business who was instrumental in pulling together the initial Video Island proposition.

Simon Morris is a marketing genius (or Chief Crazy Officer as I love to call him) who remains to this day the attitude and personality of the LOVEFiLM brand.

Mark Livingstone was the hired CEO of LOVEFiLM who led the early growth years pre the merger with Video Island in 2006.

Danny Rimer, founder and lead partner at Index Ventures, is one of the VCs who have been the catalyst and funding behind many great internet success stories including Skype and Last.fm.

George Coehlo is a senior partner at Benchmark Capital, and one of the early technology VC pioneers in Europe.

Simon Cook, partner at Cazenove PE and now senior partner at DFJ Esprit, is a real mover and shaker in the European VC community.

Thomas Hoegh is the founder of Arts Alliance Media, a family funded VC fund and the creator of the LOVEFiLM name.

Adam Valkin was the initial MD of LOVEFiLM in the early days while he was at Arts Alliance and was Thomas's right-hand man in closing acquisitions.

WHY BOARD STRUCTURE MATTERS, EVEN EARLY ON

One of the most important lessons from the early years in what became LOVEFiLM is the need to have a well-structured board that is in agreement and aligned behind the management. This may sound like the sort of corporate speak that's only relevant to larger companies, but the start-ups that succeed and manage to grow quickly are the ones with good and aligned support from a well-considered board structure. Everyone needs good external input, challenge and advice and that includes even the most stubborn and obstinate entrepreneur (and let's face it, having the courage of your convictions is an essential trait in the best entrepreneurs). Making sure that external guidance, support and advice is aligned behind the business and isn't swaying to different objectives is essential.

That was a lesson we should have learned quickly at LOVEFiLM, because the board wasn't always facing in the same direction and some early meetings were far from harmonious. And it is difficult when you have a lot of people in a boardroom at an early stage of a business trying to shape what is happening to suit their own positions. That's why entrepreneurs and anyone founding a business needs to think carefully about the make-up of their board.

When, in 2006, Video Island and LOVEFiLM combined in a 50:50 merger it created some difficulties on the board because of the personalities involved. But that merger highlighted another major success factor and that is the need to have a strong balance sheet. In the early phases it is impossible to overstate how important it is to have cash. You need to have the cash to be able to grow.

"No one should ever underestimate the importance of having cash to winning in business."

It's fair to say that Video Island was extremely well financed from the start. It had three of the top VCs in the UK invested in it and they were all keen to make it work. So it was well capitalized, and it also had a board that was aligned behind a vision to make it happen. But the cash was essential. Video Island had access to cash and no one should ever underestimate the importance of having cash to winning in business, especially in the early days when you don't know how much you'll need.

WHY SIZE MATTERS

In 2004 Video Island acquired its competitor ScreenSelect. For the first time that meant there was one company that combined good operations with cash. It meant the combined company was able to make the most of the operational advantages it had. William Reeve and Alex Chesterman, who founded ScreenSelect, had the brains to manage that business. Like some competitors they had also moved into operating white label operations for supermarkets such as Tesco.

In some ways it was this merger that created the opportunity for me to get involved. The business now had lots of different founders and funders and they wanted to bring in an external manager to run the whole business, which was where I came in. But it was an excellent and logical tie-up to combine Video Island and ScreenSelect; it was a good merger in that it brought different constituent parts there. But in those early post-merger days, in team-working parlance, it's fair to say there was a bit of "storming and norming". Different people had very different points of view. There were three board members with very robust ideas and other investors and people were looking for what was the best way to run things and they searched for which was the best idea.

Part of the change required was to bring in some truly independent advice, as well as bringing in skills to help the business grow. The good thing was that the VCs had an incredible set of contacts that allowed us to drive the business forward.

THE UPS (AND DOWNS) OF HAVING STRONG FOUNDERS

That was the good news. The not so good news was that they were the way they were because they each had very strong-willed founders and investors. That's why those early years were quite so important to the business. At this time we were trying to form and create this business and get the right board together, and get them all aligned. Essentially it was about getting the business to work together. That was quite traumatic and difficult to get through. It was hard work making sure that everyone was on board and wanted to make it work the same way.

But once you've got through that phase and it's all fixed and you've made it work, then you can be off and motoring. It is important in any business that the board and all staff are facing in the same direction and understand what they have set out to achieve, but in a start-up it is absolutely critical to be sure that everyone is aligned and agreed and heading in the same direction and wants the same things.

Some people have a very bombastic approach to board meetings in this situation, they will often shout down other people and make a lot of noise to force issues and get their own way. I hear this was how some of the very early board meetings at Video Island were. But the truth is that at such an early stage you never know which direction things will take and who you might end up getting involved with, or who might be drafted into the business by an investor. My experience is often people get involved for a period of time when they are needed and then others might get more or less involved for a time at different stages of any project. In the LOVEFiLM story this was almost Zen-like in many respects with the right people coming at just the right time. The important thing to remember is that everybody can bring different things to the business at different times, but critically you do not need everybody on the journey all the time at the same time. That is called chaos. What needs to emerge is an aligned business plan and also a structure that you can all work to. Whatever your own personal style the main point is to be yourself in the boardroom, to operate with integrity and to try not to fall out with too many people. In any market or industry you never know when paths will cross again.

WE'RE ALL IN THIS TOGETHER, EXCEPT YOU

Similarly outside of the boardroom you ultimately never know who is going to end up a good business partner and be able to help and who will not. Therefore, in the early days especially (as if you do not have enough to do) it is important to be out and about talking to everyone you can, kissing frogs so to speak, and keep your eyes and ears open for opportunities and people who might be able to help. Speak to everyone and learn as much as you can and shape up what it is you're going to do. Keep your options open and keep an open mind.

Another issue that Video Island faced after its merger with ScreenSelect was that while each of the businesses brought something positive to the table, they also brought complications. They both had different platforms, different shareholder bases (and when the LOVEFiLM element was added in, we ended up with a really fragmented and complex ownership structure), and different management and leadership styles. All of that had to be pulled together and when two small businesses come together that is difficult because spare resource to do this merger work doesn't exist and you have to somehow be totally focused on running the existing businesses and bringing them together.

For a relatively small business the combined Video Island had incredible depth of analysis available. A lot of that came from the minds and intellects of ScreenSelect founders William Reeve and Alex Chesterman and the way they managed the business. For them it was all about managing to the metrics and they built the systems that allowed them to support that. They built systems to interrogate that information to try to understand which customers were the most valuable. That approach became invaluable later on as we began to try to understand the business on a customer-by-customer basis.

By its very nature online video rental requires the business to have a really good understanding of which customers are renting which films, when and how often. But Video Island seemed to have a depth of understanding of their customers that many small businesses don't have. Indeed it understood its business better than many large corporates with endless resources at their disposal.

WHY BUSINESS MIGHT BE MORE COMPLEX THAN YOU THINK

This is the sort of issue that many would-be entrepreneurs don't think about. It's all well and good telling people that anyone can start a business, and I would be the last person to put someone off having a go, but there is a lot more to it than we sometimes say there is. If you go back to any successful business, start-up or established retail business, you'll find the people behind it understand the metrics and what's driving their business, and what they have to work on to make that business work. Often with founders it is as much intuitive as it is analyzed.

To quote Stephen Covey, these people start with the end in mind. That means asking what information you might need to track and then building the information infrastructure so that it gives you that information. And some of the simplification devices, things like the off-the-shelf accountancy packages, are interesting, but by their nature they lack the complex detail you might need. They only measure the financial results, they don't measure or track operational performance to allow you to look at things such as the lifetime value of every new customer and the cost of getting every new customer, or the conversion rate from any single marketing campaign (spend converted into new business).

"You need to know when to stop tweaking and get into the doing and growth phase. Don't let the pursuit of excellence get in the way of good enough."

At the same time there is a value in just getting on with things. The challenge is not letting this quest for information get in the way of action. You will never have a perfect information system. Even CEOs on a FTSE 100 board will tell you they don't have a perfect information system. But they have the critical information they need to run and grow the business. It is part of the challenge we all face to know when to stop collecting data or seeking perfection. Sometimes you need to know when to stop tweaking and get into the doing and growth phase. In short, don't let the pursuit of excellence get in the way of good enough.

In some ways the period up until 2004 was about the business establishing and norming. It was about getting all these different businesses under way, each one slightly different to reflect the personalities and characteristics and expertise of its founders. And where William and Alex were strong in data and metrics, the founders involved in LOVE-FiLM had a much stronger marketing bias. They also had a strong business development bias and, crucially, a strong film heritage thanks to co-founder Thomas Hoegh having worked in film production.

THE IMPORTANCE OF SAYING "YES" TO MEETINGS

My involvement with LOVEFiLM started over a coffee at the Institute of Directors. I had arranged to meet Saul Klein, who at the time was running Video Island, which had just merged with ScreenSelect. I was at something of a loose end, having just completed the turnaround at RiverDeep Plc. I caught up with Saul for a coffee and a "how's it all going?" chat. He and the VCs had been interested in hiring me into the business in 2003, but I felt it was too early and not right for me at the time. But as he told me about how the business had grown and was continuing to grow after the ScreenSelect merger, it all started to sound more interesting.

That's another thing I'd recommend. Take those off-chance meetings even if you aren't sure in advance what it will achieve or what the outcome might be. You never know where they will lead or which ones will turn out to be pivotal for you. Having met Saul and expressed an interest in getting involved with Video Island, I then went through a pretty rigorous selection process and had to present my vision for the company to the board and the founders. I got involved in working with the business early in 2005 and finally joined full time in July 2005. My adventure in LOVEFiLM was just about to start.

Lessons from a Start-up

1. **Success has many fathers, while failure is an orphan.** It may be irritating, but be prepared to recognize that it often takes several people to make a business successful.
2. **A good idea is not enough.** There are plenty of good ideas that haven't worked. You also need a range of other factors and elements to come together.
3. **Put the right talent in the right roles.** And if you don't have that, you might have to go and find it, either by recruiting someone or merging with another business that has those skills.
4. **You need an aligned board behind you**, offering external advice and support, but all facing in the same way and not out for their own ends.
5. **Don't underestimate the importance of a strong balance sheet and plenty of cash.** Every business needs cash, especially in the early stages.
6. **Don't let the pursuit of excellence get in the way of good.** While it is important to take time to get things right at the start, don't let it stop you from getting things moving. You can improve as you grow.
7. **Always be prepared to meet people**, both new people and existing contacts, because you never know where those meetings will lead.

CHAPTER 5

2005: TOWERING INFERNO

How to stop your business going up in smoke

Towering Inferno

Released: 1974

Director: John Guillermin

Cast: Steve McQueen, Paul Newman, Faye Dunaway, Fred Astaire

Synopsis: At the opening party of a colossal, but poorly constructed, office building, a massive fire breaks out that threatens to destroy the tower and everyone in it.

Awards: 3 Oscars (Cinematography, Editing, Original Song) and 2 BAFTAS (Music, Supporting Actor).

Trivia: Steve McQueen insisted that he and co-star Paul Newman had exactly the same number of lines of dialogue in the script. Both were also paid the same amount: $1 m and 7.5% of box office. Of the 57 sets built for the production, only eight remained standing when filming ended.

The phone rang at 10pm. I was staying at the salubrious North Acton Ramada Encore hotel. The voice on the other end of the line was Fern O'Sullivan, our head of operations at Video Island. She sounded calm, but concerned. "Simon," she said in a matter of fact way, "there appears to be a small fire near the distribution centre." As my hotel was only just across the road from the centre, I agreed to pop in and have a look at what was happening. To be honest, as I left the hotel, I wasn't expecting to have a great deal to do.

But as I walked over the bridge by the railway the distribution centre was about 100 yards further on. And all I could see were 40 ft flames coming out of its roof. It was a heart-stopping moment. My first reaction was, "f**k, what have I done? This business is finished." I had only joined Video Island a few months earlier. It was still so new I hadn't yet moved from Dublin back to London, hence the hotel. Now the business had apparently gone up in smoke. It transpired that a couple of Lebanese bakers had been having a feud and we appeared to get in the middle of it. At least I think that was it, rather than it being one of our rivals such as LOVEFiLM with whom we hadn't started merger discussions at that time and who were therefore still our major competitors. Either way, if anyone thought they could get rid of us that easily, they were wrong.

It was a moment when, as a relatively young and small company, survival really depends on the quality of staff and their ability to manage through a crisis. This being the early years, our distribution centre was still in the same location as the head office, but luckily it wasn't in the same building. In fact calling it a head office might be going a bit far. It was nothing so grand. It's better described as a shared facility (with bright pink floors) that happened to be adjacent to the distribution centre. It was in the old Europa Studios building in Victoria Road, North Acton, and in an effort to make it funky they had painted the floors this awful fuchsia colour. There was no air conditioning and in the summer it was stifling, while in the winter it was freezing. But it was where the business started, and in a funny way it was home.

At the same time Video Island was apparently going up in smoke in North London, LOVEFiLM was drawing on some divine intervention. It was based in a converted church at the top of the North End Road, near Earls Court, called Mission Hall. That seemed appropriate because the business didn't have any problem sorting out its mission and it certainly didn't experience the fire and pestilence that we were experiencing.

"Never underestimate how strong you and the people around you can be in a crisis."

THE POWER OF POSITIVE ACTION

Video Island's reaction to, and recovery from, the fire was remarkable. It was in hindsight a textbook example of crisis management and that was quite an achievement from such a young company. It taught me that you should never underestimate how strong you and the people around you can be in a crisis. Our response was a great example of how having an excellent senior management team makes a huge difference. The first and most important step was to determine what the impact of the fire would be. We started off by making the assumption that nothing would survive. That saved us from worrying about what we could and couldn't salvage from the ashes of the distribution centre. That made a huge psychological difference because at a single stroke the future of the business didn't depend on what we could pull out from the wreckage. We assumed not a single disc would come out in one piece.

The good news (relatively speaking) was that because we were a rental business something like 75% of our stock (i.e. the discs) was out with the customers at any one time. At that time we had almost a million discs. The challenge therefore was to be able to receive those discs out with customers, and quickly turn them around so that we could send them back out again, to keep the business moving. We got the whole management team on a call at 11pm on the night of the fire and by 2am we had agreed a plan, notified the board. We'd sent emails to every single one of our customers and suppliers and by 7am we were ready to go.

First thing that morning, with the firemen still working to put the fire out completely, we held an all-hands meeting, a sort of town hall meeting, on the steps of a nearby Lebanese restaurant (not one connected to the bakery). We were outside in the street and we told all 50 of them what had happened and our plans for how to fix it. Many were in deep shock and we had some tears but we got them all to give us their phone numbers and told them to go home because we didn't want them hanging around the area of the fire. Naturally, they all said they didn't want to go home but wanted instead to help.

The next imperative was to get some distribution capacity back up and running. With considerable effort Fern reconstructed a scaled-down version of our distribution centre in our commercial offices across the road. Bearing in mind that this was a space that was about five metres by five metres, it was quite a feat. But we set up a three-shift distribution centre in that space and sent the accountants, marketing people and editorial staff to work from home. It was an amazing achievement and within 24 hours we were already receiving discs. Customers were sending our return envelopes to the Royal Mail in Greenford who were fantastic and we needed to back up all of our post while we sorted things out. Our suppliers, the film studios and wholesalers in the industry were also incredibly helpful and they sent us new discs quickly, agreeing to sort out terms at a later date.

Within 48 hours we were also despatching discs so we were able to clear space to receive more. It was a lucky break that we had so much data to run the business that we were unable to store it onsite. With all of our data stored off-site it meant we had a sort of de facto element of a disaster recovery plan in place already and it meant we were quickly able to retrieve a functioning database.

Of course the business was insured (please get some if you don't have any) and the customers were amazing, gave us the benefit of the doubt and most stuck with us. We refunded two weeks' free subscription to everybody, which incredibly – considering what had happened – was the most we disrupted any single customer. We got new equipment and new discs and basically rebuilt the business. After surviving that, the company went on to thrive. And although it sounds odd, the fire soon became part of the legend of the company. Some employees who joined after the fire almost felt they had missed a major drama and as such missed a huge part of the history of the business.

Another important lesson from the fire was that it highlighted the need to have access to finance. We needed more cash to buy discs, and thank goodness as soon as we asked, our venture capital investors made cash available. Everyone was great and helped get the business get back onto its feet and running. Our backers were fantastic and played a great role in underwriting the business. Equally, the loss adjusters, underwriters and insurance firm were all great and the payout from the insurance came through quickly. Because we were a subscription business we were also still getting revenue through from our customer base and therefore as well as keeping them in the loop all we needed to do was compensate them with two weeks' refund on their subscription.

IT'S ALL IN THE PLAN, SO BE PREPARED TO CHANGE IT

I am a great believer in the importance of having a 100-day plan when you join a new organization. Especially when you join in the top post. Needless to say the fire totally destroyed my plan for the business. But you have to give an organization confidence that you know what you are doing and give them a vision for where you want to take it. Any 100-day plan should allow you to set out what you want to do and to give the organization a framework for your style. I also use the plan to clearly set out my expectations of them, the team I will be working with and to put out there some basic tenets and areas and how I think we will work together to deliver the plan.

As much as the fire derailed my 100-day plan, it also bizarrely helped in pulling everyone together and making it clear what we could do and what needed to be done. It also forced us to think about a new location for the distribution centre. To this day we are not entirely sure how the fire really started, but the upshot was that we faced two or three months where the business was in survival mode. It was all about managing survival. Interestingly, even though that took us back to the earliest days of being a start-up, we also had to use some big company thinking and processes. Even though the company was young we had such a lot of stakeholders and they needed to be managed. For a start by this time as well as our employees we had tens of thousands of customers, we had shareholders, a board and relationships with key members of the media.

A lot of small companies in my view don't think enough (or find the time to think) about how to manage external stakeholders. We had to merge together the small business, focused approach to just getting things done as a resource constrained team with the way things would happen at somewhere like PepsiCo. Fortunately (in hindsight), I had dealt with a lot of disaster recovery and crisis management at PepsiCo where we dealt with everything from syringes in cans to a pop star's hair catching fire.

That initial 100-day plan included two other major elements of change management. First, I believed that we needed to adjust the business model slightly and, second, we needed to get the right people into the right positions to make sure the business, and its board, were properly aligned. The distribution centre wasn't the only thing burning in the business at this time. It was also burning a lot of cash. Like many VC-funded internet start-ups, the focus had been on raising money rather than conserving or making it. The problem with this model is that no one takes enough time to focus on what each new customer brings to the business. If every new customer costs the business more than they bring in revenue, then as the business grows it will start to lose more money and will eventually need to either raise more money or go out of business.

THE POWER OF A POSITIVE CASH FLOW

At Dell I had learned a lot about measuring the cash conversion cycle. This is where the business model is set up in such a way that each new customer brings money into the business rather than costing the business money. If it is priced properly, a subscription model can work well, as members pay up front (so you have their money in advance) and not all those who sign up will use the service heavily, especially in the early days. This means that the business can have a positive cash conversion cycle.

The problem if you get that wrong is that the business can't afford the cash to grow and if you do not have access to more funding it is therefore likely to die and go bankrupt. As the leader of a business you don't want to be spending all your time and energy chasing investors for money. It is incredibly time consuming and you want to be able to focus on keeping the business going. You are also at risk of annoying existing investors who will see their stake in the business continually diluted the more external funding you get on board.

Throughout 2005 we spent a lot of time and energy getting the business model right and managing cash usage in the business and getting our cash conversion right. The model at Dell, for example, was for the company to be paid by the customer before it even placed an order. It therefore got paid before it had to pay suppliers and also before it had to pay staff. Taking the money from customers up front, the bigger the business grew, the more cash it generated. The real secret to achieving fast growth is to have a positive cash conversion cycle.

The Banks and Growing Businesses

A common complaint among small businesses in the UK is that the banks don't do enough to support them. I tend to agree. In particular there are issues about the timing of support to meet working capital requirements. Working capital is essentially the lifeblood of any firm. It determines what they can do and is essential for survival, let alone successful growth. But banks tend to be very nervous of supporting working capital. They won't lend to keep successful businesses growing. They only fund capital

(Continued)

structures where there are assets they can secure the lending against. But if a business is struggling because it doesn't have the working capital the last thing they are going to do is spend money on a piece of capital equipment. Banks needs to think about how they can get working capital funding to small firms as the business grows. Growing businesses tend to go out and raise money through equity funding rounds, which ultimately means a dilution for the people who founded the business and took the early risks. In other places there are other forms of debt that allow firms to fund working capital without being at the expense of the dilution of existing shareholders.

UK banks need to find ways to fund working capital in order to help businesses get off the ground, rather than go for equity funding or go for capital investments. These businesses don't need large capital investments. Traditionally, small firms have tended to use things like overdrafts, but they are very expensive ways of funding a business. One option is for the banks to offer what's called venture debt. That is debt in the business set up against some of the assets that attracts a higher interest rate and sometimes has warrants against it. LOVEFiLM used quite a lot of venture debt to finance the business and it was very useful. The trouble is that start-ups often don't have any assets so it is difficult to get that sort of funding in place. Which is why so many people end up securing the finance against personal assets. That might be preferable to giving up equity; it just depends on your risk profile.

IT'S GOOD TO TALK

In 2005 we also renegotiated our financial position with our bank. The business had started to do well, with new customers signing up all the time and each one now contributing positively to the company finances. There was no real need to go back to our banks or to spend as long with them as I did. But I knew that we would need them at some later point and I've always been a believer in investing time and energy in maintaining relationships when you don't need anything from the other party. It makes it much easier to approach them when you are in a position of strength. It is always easier to negotiate with banks, lenders and other suppliers when things are going well. Don't wait until you need it to start those conversations. When you think that you don't need a £500,000 overdraft is the best time to negotiate for one. It doesn't matter if you get the agreement in place and don't use it. But when you have a strong wind in your sails is the ideal time to sort out finances for the future, in case you hit stormy times. It's always better to negotiate from a position of strength rather than when you are desperate. When you are desperate you will find many doors close and suddenly your business will be at significant risk. Banks also know this and it is a game they are used to playing regularly.

"Always negotiate with banks and lenders when things are going well . . . When you are desperate you will put your business at risk."

As well as our finances I had insisted on fixing the company's board structure. As I mentioned in the previous chapter, having the right people in the right positions and creating a strong board that is well aligned in support of the executive management team is essential to the success of any young company. Given the diversity of the VC base on the board it became clear that we needed independent external board guidance. Thus we looked for and appointed a new independent chairman to lead this board change and help the business get ready for an eventual sale or flotation. The key point here is that as CEOs we often focus on what we control not what we need. Knowing who to bring in externally at what time is as important as being honest about who internally you might need to move into a different position (or even a different business altogether).

IF YOU DON'T ASK, YOU DON'T GET

I also recognized that we needed to improve our marketing. Video Island was in a fierce battle by this time with LOVEFiLM and I was always really impressed with the LOVEFiLM marketing. I knew an agency man called Philip Lay through Benchmark Capital who had worked with Simon Morris at LOVEFiLM. Simon was the man responsible for their marketing. I asked Philip to approach him to see if we could poach him. Simon unfortunately said no, LOVEFiLM had been good to him and he didn't want to move. But he's one of those true marketing geniuses who understand brands and consumer attitudes and how you communicate a proposition to consumers.

I was very keen to gather all the insight into the industry I could and I decided the best way to get that understanding was to go to the US, where Netflix had kicked off the whole DVD rental business. There is no better way to get that insight than to get it directly from the people concerned. So after an introduction from Danny Rimer (one of our VCs) I flew to America and had dinner with Reed Hastings, the founder of Netflix. At that time Netflix had just expanded 60% in one year and had some 4.5 million members. But they were very focused on the US where the competition was hotting up. They had originally planned to launch in the UK in 2005 but had pulled back as a result of this intense competition in the US and weren't looking at expanding into Europe again just yet. The conversation went something like this:

> Simon: How's it going in the US?
> Reed: Pretty good, thanks.
> Simon: When are you coming to Europe?
> Reed: Not for a while. . .
> Simon: Who do you think is going to win between Video Island and LOVEFiLM?
> Reed: I don't know, but when we get a sense for which way it is going, we'll probably try to do a deal and tie up with the winner . . .

On the flight on the way back from the US it struck me that we shouldn't allow our long-term destiny to be in the hands of another company. So when I got back I started to make overtures to the

LOVEFiLM board to say that we had to merge. I knew that the only way we would be strong enough to take on Netflix if they came into Europe was if we merged the two businesses. And while both businesses were VC backed, which should have made things easier in some respects, it actually seemed to complicate things. Partly down to the personalities of the founders and investors behind both businesses and partly due to circumstances.

Early Amazon Adventures

While in the US to meet with Netflix, I also flew to Seattle to meet with senior staff at Amazon, which was already thriving as one of the big online success stories, and which had not long before I met them launched its own video rental service. While I was there I had a meeting in a bar with Jeff Blackburn, a senior VP at Amazon. Those conversations eventually, after a number of twists and turns, led to the sale of LOVEFiLM to the US company in 2011. After the ultimate acquisition Jeff continued to be actively involved with both myself and the LOVEFiLM business, something neither of us explicitly stated back in 2005 but I suspect both privately thought.

KEEP YOUR COMPETITION CLOSE

In fact it was on that flight back home that I wrote the framework of a business plan for how we needed to merge LOVEFiLM and Video Island. Together the businesses would be able to reach critical mass. I knew that we needed to keep control of our own destiny. As long as LOVEFiLM and Video Island continued to take lumps out of each other, we were playing perfectly into the Americans' hands. The only way for us to keep control of what happened was, I felt, for the two businesses to merge.

The problem with that was that the competition between the two companies had been – and was still – fierce. The main investors of both knew each other and were always keen to get one over each other. But the Video Island founder Saul Klein's father Robin Klein introduced me to Adam Valkin. He worked closely with Thomas Hoegh, one of the key founders of LOVEFiLM. I met with Adam privately in the reception of a nice London hotel and we talked about each other's businesses. It was a frank and honest conversation.

Throughout the rest of 2005, I worked hard on both running and growing Video Island, but also on ways that the two businesses might merge. By the end the year I was ready and I took the merger proposal to the board. The response was "put together a joint business plan for what the combined business might look like". And so we set out to try to bring together the two competing businesses.

Lessons from a Crisis

1. **Never underestimate your strength in a crisis.** It can be surprising how strong you and the people around you can be when something terrible happens.
2. **Prepare all you can for the worst-case scenario.** Too often, being prepared for possible crises is seen as a luxury limited to larger companies. It should be a necessity for all organizations.
3. **Have a 100-day plan from the start.** When you join a new organization, especially in the top job, have a clear 100-day plan and stick to it. It allows you to set out what you want to do and establish a framework for your style.
4. **Have a positive cash conversion.** The real secret to achieving fast growth is to have a positive cash conversion cycle.
5. **Negotiate from strength when you can.** Speak to banks, lenders and other suppliers when things are going well. Don't wait until you need them to start those conversations.
6. **Keep control of your own destiny.** Do what you can to make sure the destiny of your business is in your own hands, even if that means taking radical action.
7. **Speak to senior industry people as often as possible.** If you want to get insight and intelligence, go directly and speak to the most senior people you can. Always ask them at the end of any meeting who else you should speak too.

Video Island and LOVEFiLM were the two main competitors in the DVD rental sector in the UK by now and had been competing against each other mercilessly for over two years. At this time I began serious conversations about actually trying to deliver a merger between the two businesses. Hmm. No prizes then for guessing why *Sleeping with the Enemy* feels like an appropriate film to represent this year.

But online DVD rental was rapidly becoming an established and accepted sector of the home entertainment industry. DVDs had almost completely taken over the home video segment in the eight years since they were launched. And that was the crucial technological development that made the mail-order video club model more viable.

THE PR WARS

Both Video Island and LOVEFiLM were proud, VC-backed businesses. Both were happy to make liberal use of the PR machine. Going at each other hammer and tongs with claim and counter-claim since 2003, there was little love lost between the two teams. Both were pushing the other hard. There was news and counter-news. LOVE-FiLM would announce it had 35,000 titles, which we suspected they did not necessarily have, so suddenly we'd announce that we had 37,500 titles. There was a sort of arms race escalation between the two firms. Although it was very amicable and friendly on the surface there was a genuine sense that this was the opposition and these were the people we were competing against.

This sense of competition was stoked by the fact that the founders and funders were proud, and some would say mischievous, people. This competition was played out in the press. But the upside of this was that both businesses benefited from the hostilities, because thanks to the press coverage it meant we were constantly raising awareness of our services. Whether it was a discussion about ScreenSelect or LOVEFiLM it all helped boost awareness and grow subscribers. Importantly it also gave both businesses an external focus that helped keep both moving forward at a pace and accelerated innovation.

When we decided to bring the two businesses together my energies were naturally focused for a while on getting the deal done and then on the post-merger integration of the two businesses. On paper it seemed an obvious deal to do. Video Island (with ScreenSelect) at this stage had the money and the best operational platform, while LOVE-FiLM had the best marketing and by far the strongest consumer brand. I also felt that bringing the consumer brand and the company name together was an obvious win.

In order to get the deal together I spent a lot of time with Adam Valkin, who headed up the negotiations for LOVEFiLM. All the way through the merger process there were countless times when I thought that the deal was going to collapse or not happen. There were numerous occasions when it nearly didn't go through. We all had to be tenacious and believe that what we were doing was right, which certainly Adam and I did.

LET THE MERGER BEGIN

It was challenging for me as the outgoing CEO of Video Island, looking after the Video Island shareholders and knowing I was going to be CEO of the new LOVEFiLM entity and have responsibilities to a doubly large group of shareholders as well. I had to manage through that. Working with Adam was very straightforward. He was a pragmatic, straight and very smart guy and we managed to get most of the issues sorted easily. Then it became a matter of making it work and integrating the two teams and the different systems.

The good news was that when we first sat down with one another we were fairly close. We had established some key principles in advance. So, the deal was always going to be a 50:50 merger. We agreed not to try to horse trade on a little value here and there. Both companies had obvious strengths and weaknesses, both financial and operational, and so on. We could put in warranties to cover some eventualities if things didn't work, but overall we had to recognize the logic that the sum of the parts was going to be a lot greater.

While Adam and I were both quite aligned all along, what we both had to do was take that attitude and belief back to our boards and sell the merger deal to them. And what neither side wanted was to feel they were being screwed. As always, we ended up with everyone feeling a little bit compromised. It was one of those situations where we had to share the perceived pain out equally to enjoy the real long-term gains. The idea was that the upside from the power and strength of the combined operation would be a lot better.

One thing that was unusual about the deal was that both sides appointed the same corporate finance advisor, Altium. That was very strange, but it meant we didn't have me and Adam sat in one room discussing the deal, with bankers and lawyers sitting in other rooms arguing about details of the deal. Altium's role was to help bridge the gap between both sides as a sort of corporate finance arbitration service. We both gave lots of confidential information to them and they were able to provide comprehensive independent financial assessments of both businesses. And they could compare the differences between the two businesses?

Top Tips on How to Do a Deal

Getting deals done and pushing through the process is in my view all about deal momentum. You have to keep conversations going. You can't leave anything to lie for too long, it has to keep moving and you have to keep up the pressure to do a deal and resolve issues with the individuals involved. It's also the same when you are hiring people. It's important to keep the process moving.

We used a novel, innovative way of doing the deal, with the same advisor for both sides. In truth lots of discussions happen between VC-backed firms, but not all that many mergers happen between them. I think having an initial agreement to the basic principles in place is important if possible, and choosing and totally trusting the right advisors also makes a huge difference. And it requires lots of late-night working. You just have to put the hours in to get these deals done.

BE PREPARED TO WORK HARD TO SECURE THE DEAL

We had to keep the deal totally confidential within the two businesses. Only a limited number of people on both sides knew anything about it. The deal was called Project Cupid on the Video Island side and Project Zulu at LOVEFiLM. But keeping that all-important deal momentum going is essential. And it requires lots of late-night working. You just have to put the hours in to get these deals done. I'll never forget that the day the deal was signed was the day of my grandmother's funeral. It meant that I didn't go to her funeral, which I bitterly regret to this day. When you are working until 4 o'clock in the morning trying to get a deal done as quickly as expected, it is bound to have an impact on your personal life.

However much you prepare in advance and expect things to go a certain way, these deals often end up taking longer and being more complex than expected. This was certainly true here. It was a lot more complex than I expected. One added complication was that Thomas Hoegh's company, Arts Alliance and Media, which was the selling shareholder on the LOVEFiLM side, wanted to retain the rights to the download capability that LOVEFiLM used. So we had a separate contractual agreement on the side for that, which took up a lot of time. Further down the line it was ripped up because the service wasn't good enough for our customers. But that alone took weeks to negotiate and do. The total value of the deal quoted in the press at the time was £60m.

Part of the challenge of the early Video Island days was that the investors had a preference share structure, which meant that they would get their money out first and what was left would be split among the rest. In a way, if they put money in they were getting it out twice. They would argue that it was fair because they were taking the risk and investing the money. And the management would say they were taking risks and investing time and resource and energy.

One of the things we had to do at Video Island to make the merger work was get to a common share structure where one share was equal

"Having the right share structure was vital in getting everyone aligned, from the management to the board to the external investors."

to one share. So we increased the total number of shares and those with preference shares got paid a premium for those shares and that managed to level itself out. This meant that when we merged the two businesses it could be a straight 50:50 merger, with one share equalling one share for everyone. That was the right thing to do and helped us to get a deal done, and I have to thank George Coehlo from Benchmark (now Balderton) for taking the tricky lead with the VCs on this discussion.

There was something like over 50 investors. Everyone supported the deal because financially, logically and intellectually it made sense. It was an inevitable consolidation in the industry. But it meant that the people who were involved in the initial idea were seeing their share reduced. Which is difficult to swallow, until you realize that you are getting a smaller slice of a much bigger pie with much more growth potential. It just made sense.

Having the right share structure was vital in getting everyone aligned, from the management to the board to the external investors. We didn't want anyone to be enemies, we all had to be lined up and facing the same way. We then had to move to a new office.

"YOU WANT ME TO WORK WITH *THEM*?"

The merger deal was completed in April 2006. And when it was finally done there was a real sense of relief and celebration. Once the deal was cleared by regulators and went ahead we called everyone together into town hall meetings at both companies. While everyone could see the sense in what we were doing, the competition between the two rival firms had been fierce and I think there were some people feeling "oh my God, I've got to work with these other people".

That's where the post-merger leadership and integration work needed to come into its own. I worked very closely with the then LOVEFiLM

CEO Mark Livingstone, who is a great talent and had been a key part in the company's early success. He also made it clear from the start that he didn't want to run the combined organization, so we weren't competing for the same job and we were able to work very closely to ensure that the communication was smooth, consistent and comprehensive. Everything was scripted and carefully managed and we had HR and legal support on hand to manage the changes and any questions.

We set ourselves a goal of getting the whole transition done as quickly as possible, within 90 days, and moved all the staff initially to the Video Island offices. These were horrible offices and that is why we quickly found somewhere else. A new, fresh, joint space was important as it represented a fresh start for both companies. To this day I still tell Simon Morris, the LOVEFiLM marketing leader who turned us down before, that we did the deal to eventually get him into the business, although it was a bit of an extreme way of doing it.

THE BUSINESS OF INTEGRATION

The rest of 2006 was therefore all about merging and integrating the two businesses, defining a new culture and behaviours and ensuring that the new team that worked together worked together effectively as a team.

Because I had only been at Video Island less than a year, people didn't really see me as coming from one side or the other. And right from the start I defined which team I wanted, what I wanted them to do and how I wanted them to work together. That meant a mix of Video Island staff, LOVEFiLM staff and some new blood. So I hired Jim Buckle as CFO and Andrew Ground as UK managing director. That meant we had a really good balance of Video Island, LOVEFiLM and great new blood in the new team.

There were at times some slightly awkward moments post-merger, when there were discussions about which platform to use or which managers should lead part of the organization. Naturally there was a bit of bias by managers towards their previous companies' personnel or systems but we needed to work through this. But the important thing in these situations is just to make a decision; getting the right decision is obviously preferable, but often with imperfect information the key is not to be ambiguous or uncertain for too long.

Decision Making in Large and Small Companies

This reminds me that it is worth noting some of the differences between small and large companies when it comes to making decisions. In large companies you can often afford to procrastinate. In small companies you can't. If you don't decide something a small business might be paralyzed. You often can't move on until a decision is made. This can help drive a business forward and maintain momentum. Large companies can usually carry on regardless while a decision is referred all the way up the chain of command to the top. In small firms you need the momentum and you need decisions being made all the time. When people join small companies from large organizations this speed of decision making can catch them out. They are used to writing a discussion paper or having "talks about talks", to use that expression from the Northern Ireland peace process. In a small business there isn't the luxury of time or the resources required to analyze and review every decision over and over. You have to think fast, act faster and then move on. It's a good discipline to learn and it's something more people in large companies could benefit from learning from their small business counterparts.

Although the bulk of both businesses was UK focused, both had also acquired related operations in Scandinavia. Video Island acquired BraFilm in Norway and Sweden and LOVEFiLM had acquired a company in Denmark called Digitarian and a company in Sweden called Boxman. So part of the challenge of merging the businesses was how we could also merge the Scandinavian businesses. I therefore picked the most senior LOVEFiLM person in Sweden, a guy who I thought was the most experienced. However, he proved to be the wrong person. It wasn't that I didn't think that Jonas and Magnus who founded BraFilm weren't fantastic, because they were. But I needed someone to take the lead and I thought my choice had the best skills and expertise for the combined role. It took us a while to recover from that in those markets.

"Good leaders spot their mistakes quickly, admit them, adjust their thinking and move on."

With hindsight I should have taken a different call. The key lesson in this case is to spot mistakes quickly, admit them and adjust and move on. I hadn't chosen the right person for the job. Part of my decision was probably that he was a counter-balance, because he came from the LOVEFiLM side, and I didn't want a Video Island person in charge in every location. It was the wrong call and it hurt us. We didn't move on as quickly as we could have, because I left the situation alone, even when I knew there was a problem. That was because I was keen to retain stability while we set about making the UK merger work, as this was where the vast majority of our subscribers were. The situation was compounded because at the same time we were merging all the businesses onto a single platform in Sweden we had the biggest marketing push for new customers we'd ever had there. So all these new customers joined just as we were transitioning the platform. On reflection we also shouldn't have had that marketing push when we did. But we wanted to be ready for it. It often happens that way. You build up your marketing activity based on the idea that you'll have the platform migration done first before any of the marketing activity, but then the technology means that the migration gets delayed and then it's too late and you are locked into the marketing activity. We almost doubled the number of subscribers with that promotion, and we couldn't keep up with the pace of change in the business. As a result we suffered some bad customer experiences and ended up with a *WatchDog*-style investigation of BraFilm on TV.

BUILD VALUES WITH YOUR CUSTOMERS IN MIND

That was a huge learning about always keeping your eye on the customers. Now, whenever we have technology changes or platform migrations we always look to see what marketing we have planned and ask how can we stop or delay it to ensure we are all working in sync.

An essential part of bringing the two businesses together was instilling a set of values and beliefs in the business.

The LOVEFiLM Values

Innovation
Loving customers
Being an all-star cast
Making sure we were famous for the right stuff
Passion

We also had a set of principles for consumers in terms of how we run the business and what it is about. We decided that whatever we did we would always seek to offer **Value, Choice and Convenience**.

There is a tendency to see values and mission statements as fluff. But the most important thing for me is not the absolute detail of the words of a set of values, but how you interpret them into day-to-day behaviours as a management team and how you live your life to them. Paying vision and strategic mission consultants hundreds of thousands of pounds to work that out can, in my view, be a waste of money. Your organization knows what is important and what's not. Sit down with your teams and discuss what they consider important, take lots of notes and pull out the key themes that emerge. You must be genuine to the people and culture that you already have.

Values from other companies are also good to look at during this process to check you haven't missed anything off. Most large public companies have these displayed on their own websites for the world to see, so why not learn as a small company from the money they have already spent? For me, the most important thing is the values. Once you have the values lined up and you, as a management team, are living these values then you can change the vision or direction more easily. That was important because at LOVEFiLM in those early years the nature and direction of what we were doing was changing on an almost quarterly basis, but we knew the values we built in 2006 remained the same and they are still in the company today.

Of course the merger process meant we had to get rid of some people where there was overlap. Getting rid of people is never an easy thing to do. The only approach to take is to treat everyone fairly all the time. As long as you do that, that should be the end of it; say goodbye to them properly and thank them for all of their support but move on. But never shy away from making those decisions. You can offer help, support and training. But it's also important to get involved and do it yourself. Don't outsource those difficult conversations. As I mentioned earlier, when I worked as a consultant I had been flown in to an insurance company to lay off half of its independent financial advisors. Even as a young man I felt it was wrong to get an outsider to do that job.

FOCUS ON THE SURVIVORS

But it's most important to spend time thinking about the people who are staying. At a time of change it is easy to focus on the people who are leaving and forget about the people staying, who actually are the ones who most need your attention. Don't forget those who are staying.

"At a time of change it is easy to focus on the people who are leaving and forget about the people staying, who actually are the ones who most need your attention."

Because the two businesses were so different and had different cultures, it was important that we forged a strong culture and a clearly defined set of values for the combined company. Video Island was very operational, very metrics and data driven, while LOVEFiLM was very brand and marketing focused and very studio driven. The challenge was to bring together the best elements of both businesses and make sure the combined business was better than the sum of its parts. We put in place some strong cultural values and markers and tried to create a business that represented the best of both worlds.

It was important to get everyone operating on 30-, 60- and 90-day integration plans. We had this whole cycle of everyone in the business working on a quarterly performance review. We kept the best people, lost a few where there was overlap, and then we were off, growing and recruiting to fill the skill gaps where we identified them.

We wanted new offices so that no one was living in "the enemy's" office. It had to be a new LOVEFiLM space, neutral to what had gone previously for either side. We picked North Acton. It was cheap, but we made it our own and made it quite funky, entrepreneurial and new-tech.

By August/September we had the two businesses integrated, the two back-end platforms properly integrated and we were working off one customer database. The challenge now became how to grow this newly combined venture.

At this stage we also hired a new, independent chairman. That was when Charles Gurassa came on board. At that point we had four VCs on the board. And each would have his or her point of view. In fairness, the four worked together pretty well on the whole and agreed about most things, but having an independent chairman really helped both the business and me.

Lessons from a Growing Business

1. **Good leaders spot their own mistakes quickly,** admit to them, adjust their thinking, make any required changes and move on.

2. **Keep your eye on your customers at all times,** but especially at times of change. It may sound trite, but change often makes people focus internally and lose sight of their customers.

3. **During times of change, focus your attention on the employees staying.** Any restructuring means you will lose people, and too much attention goes to those who leave. Don't forget those staying behind. They are the future, so focus on them.

4. **Appoint someone independent to lead your board.** An external view and balance can make all the difference when times get tough.

5. **An organization's values should come from within,** not from external consultants. Employees know what's important to them and what's not, so sit down with them, hold meetings and talk about what matters and pull out themes.

6. **Don't shy away from or outsource difficult conversations.** It's important to get involved and handle them yourself.

7. **Take time to get your share structure right.** It is vital in getting everyone aligned, from the management to the board to the external investors.

CHAPTER 7
2007: BRAVEHEART

Bet big or go home

Braveheart

Released: 1995

Director: Mel Gibson

Cast: Mel Gibson, Sophie Marceau

Synopsis: The story of William Wallace, a 13th century Scottish warrior who gained recognition when he came to the forefront of the First War of Scottish Independence by opposing King Edward I of England.

Awards: 5 Oscars (Best Picture, Best Cinematography, Best Director, Best Sound Editing, Best Makeup) and 3 BAFTAS (Best Cinematography, Best Costume Design, Best Sound).

Trivia: Real-life Wallaces appear as extras in the movie and Mel Gibson also stayed with them during the filming, in order to learn more about the history. The only way Gibson could get the film made in the first place was by agreeing with Paramount Studios that he would also star in the film.

There's a lot of debate about the defining characteristics of entre-preneurs and whether they are born or made. And this isn't the place to attempt to offer a definitive answer to either question. But one trait commonly cited as marking out entrepreneurs is their attitude to risk. Entrepreneurs are seen as big risk takers. Leaders in large cor-porates, by contrast, are perceived as tending toward taking the safe and the conservative option, weighing up possible impacts and out-comes and taking slower, safer decisions as a result.

I would question this characterization. I don't think attitudes to risk are as clear-cut as this approach suggests. It's true that I know several entrepreneurs who have taken huge gambles without even blinking. But it's not that they seek out risk, it's more that they just don't stop to consider the possible downsides. It simply doesn't figure in their thinking. In other words, rather than seeing risks and bravely soldier-ing on, they simply don't perceive risks others might.

This can be put down to a combination of personality traits that include high self-confidence and low self-esteem. Their confidence means they approach new projects with a positive attitude but they are also driven by a need to achieve often as a result of low self-esteem. This leads to them feeling pressurized to make things work. Often there is too much personal emotional capital invested in a project to allow it to fail. Thus they achieve apparently superhuman feats of success, often against the odds, by seeming to take those high-risk gambles.

EMPTYING THE BANK TO BET BIG

In the LOVEFiLM story there is a point at which we took a huge gamble. Having combined and realigned the businesses into a single, strong entity, drawing on the best of all three key founding businesses, and having made sure that the business would be cash generative as it grew, we decided to go all out to achieve that growth.

It's important to remember that because of the nature of all three businesses we had a boardroom full of hungry, aggressive, go-getting venture capitalists. It was no surprise therefore that they were always keen to take the business on to the next level as quickly as possible. There was always a positive pressure to look out for the next deal. That probably explains why the business accelerated from a standing start to a significant sale in less than a decade.

At the end of 2006, we decided that the way to do that would be to get the brand name in front of more people. At the end of 2006 we had tested some TV advertising in Scotland. The results, although marginal in isolation, were good enough to convince us to take the campaign forward and go nationwide. The Scottish results were such that we knew we would attract enough new customers to cover the cost of the campaign. Rolled out nationally, with the benefit of scale in our costs, it was clear that the argument in favour appeared to stack up even more. But the thing about marketing, and above-the-line advertising in particular, is that you never know which way it is going to turn out and what will work and what will bomb. There's a famous quote variously attributed to US retail pioneer John Wanamaker and, more pertinently given my early career, to William Hesketh Lever, along the lines of "I know that only half my marketing works, the trouble is I don't know which half." I'd already experienced this at Pepsi, where the PepsiMax campaign, which was almost entirely lifted from another Pepsi-owned drink brand, had won all sorts of awards.

At the start of 2007, LOVEFiLM had about £2.5 m in its bank account. It wasn't a bad situation to be in, but the TV campaign we were looking at was going to cost £2 m. It was a massive gamble. It's one of the riskiest moves I have made in my business career. It wasn't complete make or break if the campaign bombed but it would severely hamper our ability to grow. We might have be able to carry on growing, but it would be at a much slower rate. But I knew that even with the support of the VCs on the board the only way to achieve the growth I wanted was to bet on this campaign. That's why I chose *Braveheart* as the film of 2007.

Even though it was a gamble, we did what we could to stack the odds in our favour. The campaign was grounded in a lot of research and a rich and detailed understanding of our customers. This was another example of how having the right people in the right positions really makes a difference. We had Andrew Ground as UK managing director and he was second to none in building consumer insight and understanding how customers actually behaved and would react to various initiatives. Andrew, with his Cambridge degree in mathematics, led some great modelling that meant we were able to see that the TV campaign as tested in Scotland lost us a little, in that we were spending more acquiring customers than they spent once they joined. But we knew that when it was rolled out nationally the revenue per customer acquired would be much higher than the cost of acquiring them, so it was worth doing.

TAKE SMALL, SURVIVABLE RISKS

This is where it gets back to the attitude to risk. It shows how smaller businesses can learn from larger businesses. Of course, you will never have perfect information and at some point you have to take a call and give something a go. But there is no reason, regardless of size, not to weigh up all available information and reduce the risk as far as possible. We were in a position to be able to conduct a small-scale trial in a test market and I'd recommend this wherever possible. Try things out on a small scale before launching to the wider market as a whole. If something isn't going to work, you don't want it potentially damaging your brand, especially if it's not that strong.

Way back at Unilever, I worked on the launch of what became the first Persil fabrics washing liquid. Rather than risk damaging the Persil brand, Unilever went as far as creating a new brand called Wisk. Only when the liquid concept was tested and proven did we then launch a Persil fabrics washing liquid. This is an extreme example, but the principle of doing all you can to reduce unnecessary risk to a brand remains the same for all businesses. It takes a lot to build a brand and very little to destroy one especially with the increased influence of social media and micro-blogging sites giving more power to the customers' voice. It is important to do as much as you can to protect your brand.

THE POWER OF CREATIVE THINKING

Of course it also helps to have a maverick genius devising and overseeing your marketing. We were lucky to have Simon Morris heading that up for us. It reduced the risk of the campaign significantly. Simon is one of those rare talents you come across from time to time. He created this amazing TV ad and even convinced Ewan McGregor to do the voiceover, and frankly we "blew the doors off" with this massive £2m advertising campaign. The campaign was a massive hit and it transformed awareness of LOVEFiLM.

It had been a big bet, but I had had plenty of support from the board. This is the sort of gamble for growth that plays well to the culture of VCs. Venture capital investment is all about achieving scale and how big you can grow a business quickly. Huge growth, as long as it's sustainable, is nearly always lucrative. So there was support from them in doing it from the start. As a result of that campaign people in the media, in the public and in business started to talk about LOVEFiLM. We had established the business.

From that moment on LOVEFiLM became a different business, because it became a household name. The external perception had always been that we were a lot bigger than we really were. At these early stages we were still a low-key, entrepreneurial, let's all muck in together kind of a business. But the key thing from this campaign was that it ignited the public's passion and interest in the brand. And I have always worked and enjoyed working in businesses where people have a strong passion and affection for the brand. My latest role at Mothercare is another great example of that. I wouldn't be interested if people didn't talk about it with a passion. The times in my career I have found it hardest to do my job is where I didn't relate to the product as a consumer as much. Dell, with its server and storage stacks for business, would be a good example of this.

A PAIN IN THE NORDICS

Around this time I finally got my act together and dealt with the underperforming Nordic business. I had let it go on for too long. As a leader, if someone is not performing in your organization, it is really important that you act and are seen to act. The chances are that the rest of the organization knows well before you do what is happening and that this one person isn't working. It's important not to be too proud to think that because you make a decision you have to stick with it. Be prepared to hold your hands up and admit a mistake. Make the change and move on. And make it as quickly as possible. Clearly I didn't do that in this case.

Of course it's more difficult when your mistake is that you let go someone you should have kept in the business. I would put allowing Alex Chesterman, one of the founders of ScreenSelect, to leave into that category. Alex is one of the greatest business development people I have ever worked with. He was one of the sharpest commercial guys I've met and it's no surprise that he has gone on to enjoy huge success founding Zoopla. But there was tension between him and a lot of other members of the board and we took the opportunity to have a discussion with him when we merged with LOVEFiLM and he agreed he would go and not be part of the new world.

But when things go wrong it is important as a leader to hold your hand up and take responsibility. It is sometimes difficult to separate out responsibility and accountability. But if you are accountable for something you want to be responsible for what happens. No one gets it right all the time. When the rest of the team see you admitting mistakes it also begins to change the culture a bit, suddenly it is less of an issue to fail and staff begin to take a few more risks, pushing the boundaries a bit more themselves. As long as people learn from these mistakes, of course, then it can be a very powerful advantage.

ALTERNATIVE APPROACHES TO FINANCE

The other big lesson from 2007 was how we funded the business. Thanks to some great marketing, a huge word of mouth buzz and offering a consistently good service to a loyal customer base, we were growing at a staggering rate. Despite having a positive cash conversion cycle, getting ready and responding to that type of exponential growth required money and needed to be properly funded. So rather than dilute the equity holding of existing shareholders and complicate the ownership structure any further, we opted to take on debt rather than look at more equity finance. The desire not to dilute the shareholdings any more meant we had to look at the other assets the business owned and to see what we could do to raise finance against them. We realized that our biggest asset was our DVD library and so we secured the debt against that library.

This sort of so-called "venture debt" can be a great way to get cash relatively quickly, but it isn't cheap. We took that bond finance and that bond had certain warrants or some equity against the company as part of its return. We raised £10 m that way and they did very well out of it. The gamble allowed us to get the customers and grow, but in order to fund that growth and get more discs in we needed the extra working capital that the venture debt released. That money again transformed the business at the growth rates we were achieving and allowed us to kick on and really accelerate our growth.

Why Start-ups are Scared of Equity Finance

What start-ups tend to do very early on is to use friends' and families' or their own money and then as they grow they turn to more established businesses such as VCs, or if they are in positive cash flow they go to the banks. Banks support asset investment, not working capital investment, and what most businesses need is working capital investment. Venture debt can become useful at times as you do not need to give up a significant number of shares or a lot of equity in your business to get cash. Typically for this, what such providers want is a higher interest rate vs the

(Continued)

bank and some warrants (similar to share options with a fixed entry price) all secured against some assets that you may have. For us at LOVEFiLM our major assets were the DVD library we had so we were able to use this at a time before we made any profits which is what the banks demanded before they would lend us anything. It is in the VCs' interest to put cash in because as the business becomes more valuable they own more of it. As far as we were concerned it shows you that the VCs were willing to work with us because Simon Cook, one of our leading and most supportive VC partners, introduced us to Ross at Kreos to help us get that venture debt funding. So they often did what was best for the business not just what was in their short-term interest. This may be rare, but it was our experience. The key lesson from all this fundraising and the activity of the VCs on the board was that it's vital to pick your partners carefully. Too often people in need of finance or looking to complete a merger or acquisition don't invest enough time in properly assessing the partners they want to do that work for them and with them. But it is crucial to get that right.

Lessons from an Emerging Brand

1. **Sometimes you have to bet big,** in order to win anything worthwhile.
2. **Controlled risk taking is good for business, reckless gambles are not.** A positive attitude to risk doesn't mean you can't do all you can to reduce the chance of failure.
3. **It's impossible to overstate the importance of brand awareness for consumer brands.** Always spend as much as you can afford on targeted marketing that raises your brand profile but be ready for it if it takes off.
4. **There are more ways to fund a business than you imagine.** Look at other ways to fund business growth than simple bank lending or giving away equity.
5. **Make the effort to understand difficult people.** Getting rid of star performers can be an expensive mistake. Stars can be difficult to manage, but sometimes it's worth the effort if they can stay true to your behaviours and values.
6. **Have the courage to act quickly to get rid of people who aren't performing.** The sooner it's done, the better for all parties.
7. **Your teams will learn it is OK to fail if you admit your own mistakes.** Be brave and put your hands up when you get it wrong, they will support you even more and take more risks themselves.

CHAPTER 8
2008: THE GODFATHER

Kissing frogs and kicking tyres

The Godfather

Released: 1972

Director: Francis Ford Coppola

Cast: Marlon Brando, Al Pacino, James Caan

Synopsis: The aging patriarch of an organized crime dynasty transfers control of his clandestine empire to his reluctant son.

Awards: 3 Oscars (Best Actor, Best Picture, Best Writing)

Trivia: Marlon Brando refused to accept his Oscar because of Hollywood's discrimination against Native American people. The early buzz on the film was so positive that a sequel was planned before the first one had finished filming. Marlon Brando didn't memorize his lines and read from cue cards during most of the film.

By 2008 the business was flying. All the early issues around integration had been resolved and we'd created an organization with a powerful culture built on high performance and a dedication to excellent customer service. The advertising campaign had helped us establish the brand as a household name. But in some ways getting customers is the easy part. Keeping them is much harder, especially in a fiercely competitive market. I had to make sure that everyone in the business, regardless of whether or not they dealt with customers directly, was focused on doing what they could to improve the customer experience.

From very early on, when it was still a small business, there was a strong performance review system in place. It's the kind of thing that is easy not to bother with, especially when there aren't many people in the business. But it's well worth putting in place. We had a system of quarterly performance reviews, which I go into in more detail in the next chapter. For the moment it's enough to know that two main benefits of this system were that it allowed the managers in the business to manage. I find the old debates about the difference between leadership and management a little odd. The distinction between the two is clear enough for me. Leaders provide the vision and set the direction and objectives, including setting the organizational structure and defining the key tasks, roles and responsibilities within that.

ALLOWING MANAGERS TO MANAGE

Managers are then responsible for making things happen, for organizing people and resources in such a way as to make sure that the goals and objectives are achieved. This includes regular monitoring and measurement of everyone's performance (preferably on a quarterly basis) so that high achievers can be rewarded and any poor performance can be spotted early and dealt with quickly. It gets back to one of my mantras, that it's impossible to effectively run an organization unless you are on top of the key metrics. Knowing the vital statistics of your business is essential and that includes the key performance measures for all staff.

All this meant that it became obvious in 2008 that not all parts of the business were performing to an equal standard. Put simply, by the measures we had in place it was clear that the business wasn't succeeding equally everywhere. It was tough to get stuff done in some places. We weren't the largest of organizations and yet we seemed to be making the same mistakes in one region that we had already made elsewhere. We just weren't learning across the organization.

MORE PAIN IN THE NORDICS

It was an issue that to some extent I had created. I had structured the organization at the time we merged with LOVEFiLM into regions and each region had all of the functions underneath it and there were regional heads. The problem was we weren't big enough to make this work. We didn't have the scale to have the critical mass in each functional area or, as the jobs were not big enough, to attract the right talent into each region. As a result we were inefficient and struggling. So I had to act quickly and be quite ruthless about it. I collapsed down the regions and rearranged the whole organization into a functional structure. The Nordic region had been problematic since the merger. I had already had to get rid of the regional head once and now I had to do it again. But while effective leaders need to be aware of the softer people skills and be emotionally engaged, it's also important to be seen to be decisive and to act quickly. One of the reasons I chose *The Godfather* for this year is while I wouldn't say I modelled my approach on Marlon Brando's by any stretch of the imagination, to make the business successful we had to act swiftly to clear out a lot of dead wood and rebuild. Recognizing when you haven't got it right is half the battle and taking swift action to remedy the situation is the other.

This is where the performance review system comes in handy. You get a very regular pulse from around the business of what's working and what isn't. The key learning is the importance of listening to people in the business and getting out there and meeting them and experiencing what they are saying and hearing for yourself that things are not working. If you take time with them and they begin to trust you, then people will tell you when things are not working and when they are struggling to get the things done they want to do. In the Nordic region people were asking why, if we're doing things right in the UK, are we not doing those things in Germany or the Nordics and vice versa?

KICKING THE TYRES

While internally we were making tough calls to make sure we maintained high performance, the outside world was beginning to sit up and take notice of LOVEFiLM. And that naturally meant that around this time we had a number of very flattering encounters with some of the largest companies in the world. It was obvious to anyone with half a business brain that the structure of LOVEFiLM, with its history and board chocked full of VCs, meant that it was going to be up for sale at some stage. From fairly early on we got a steady stream of suitors coming to start conversations with us and wanting to have a look around. These included a large, international news and entertainment corporation, as well as a very powerful and wealthy global internet company.

This is the second reason why *The Godfather* seemed very appropriate for this year. We were getting the so-called "offers we couldn't refuse" and by now you know what we did, which was the right thing to do. In this situation we quickly learned that there was an element of what people in the motor trade call "tyre kicking", that is to say people coming around to have a good look at the business but who were only half-hearted in their interest. They wanted to have a good nose into the business, but they either weren't serious or weren't the right people in that business to make the decisions. It is very easy to get your head turned and be seduced when a big name from a powerful company wants to meet you. The important things in this situation are to ascertain as quickly as possible how serious they are and also not to be overwhelmed by them. LOVEFiLM was also quite good at punching above its weight and appearing much bigger and more powerful than we really were.

Of course with the board we were all already thinking about the right exit. There are only a couple of
negotiation points where as a VC you can realize
real value and the key one of those is the exit,
whether that is a trade sale or flotation (the other
by the way is the deal you do on entry). The business
we were in, especially in 2008 as the digital development really started to gain momentum, was one that
required deep pockets.

"It was a simple matter of numbers. If we kissed enough frogs, one of them might turn out to be a prince."

That meant that when those big multinational organizations came
calling, even if they were tyre kicking, we had to be open to them. It's
always possible, especially when you are in competition, that they are
there just to learn from you and extract information about the way
you do things. That's not meant to sound arrogant, but any new,
young and innovative company will have things they do that can be
very attractive to an older, more established organization. But even
so, the unfortunate thing was that with an exit in mind, we had to
talk to them. For our investors it was a simple matter of numbers. If
we kissed enough frogs, one of them might turn out to be a prince.

While they can be time-consuming and distracting it is also possible,
if you approach it properly, to use these meetings to learn about the
larger companies and for it to be a useful catalyst to trigger thinking
about how you approach things in your own business. Don't be afraid
to use these meetings for your own benefit. You might not be as close
to some areas of the market or new thinking. So these meetings can
be a great source of new ideas, new ventures and new products or
services. If you think about why they want your business and how it
might fit into their existing model, you can begin to see how they are
thinking. This can sometimes help you clarify how you might go about
acquiring new content or launching new devices or approaching your
digital offering. But it can equally be a lot of time wasting and a bit
of a distraction. I guess it's like anything. If a deal happens it is the
best time you ever invested, but generally it is just a drain on your
scarce resources and a waste of time.

Checklist for Speaking to Potential Buyers

If you are in the position of being courted by potential new owners, you have to put yourself in their shoes. Think about how your business could fit into theirs and about the potential synergies, as well as the opportunities and overlaps. Look at all the assets that the company has and how you might fit into those assets. Is there a logical fit between their business and yours? Thinking about this can help you to see their strategy more clearly. There is a checklist that you look at if someone approaches you:

1. Does the story stack up for them as much as it does for you? If it doesn't, the chances are they are just wasting your time and trying to find out information about you that will benefit them.
2. Do they have the financial bandwidth to be able to make the acquisition? If they don't, again the chances are there is something else going on.
3. Are you speaking to the right people or are these people lower down the food chain, and not the decision makers? We went a long way with a worldwide technology company and there was a lot of interest. They had another video business and we could see how the two would fit together, but it turned out we weren't there with the ultimate decision makers.

As early as 2005 I had been in touch with Amazon, which was even then starting to get into the DVD rental business itself. Despite its resources, it realized that the offering and systems and processes for doing it well are more complex than they appear. In 2008, with the tyre kicking from large global businesses going on, it was inevitable that we'd carry on those conversations with Amazon. The difference with Amazon was that we both had something of interest to the other party. Sure they wanted to get involved with our business, not least because they recognized we could improve the experience for the Amazon video customers. They also could see that we were developing a powerful physical/digital hybrid business model that fitted well with their own approach. Even though we hadn't got the digital side completely right, they could see we were investing in it. And we liked the people there, too.

AMAZON COMES CALLING

So when Amazon came knocking we were keen to speak to them. Eventually we agreed on a complex deal that involved them getting some equity and a seat on the board in exchange for some cash, their entire DVD rental customer base (who would all become LOVEFiLM customers) and a two-year marketing deal. So Amazon became a shareholder in the business, got a seat on the board and we got their DVD rental business and transitioned all Amazon rental customers into LOVEFiLM customers – they were also going to lend us some of their marketing muscle. It was my kind of deal because it was a win for Amazon, for everyone at LOVEFiLM and for our customers (as well as the Amazon customers).

But before the deal could be completed we were subject to an Office of Fair Trading investigation. This time it was because LOVEFiLM was getting big enough to be noticed and Amazon was obviously a big player.

As part of the OFT investigation and our response to it, we had to interrogate every email sent over the past five years. I was very concerned about it at the time because I really wanted the deal to go through. I knew it would be good for consumers as well as good for us as a business. It was a great deal for everyone and I didn't feel there should be any competition issues or market distortion at all. And as well as the investigation being very expensive, it was very distracting and time-consuming for senior management. There's also the organizational strain, having announced something you have everyone aligned and ready, but you have to wait before you can get on with the integration. It's often in the confusion gap caused by the hold-up that competitors start to come in and do more aggressive marketing, even if they themselves may have triggered the investigation.

In the end we didn't get referred, but the defence cost us over £1m. Yes, that shocked me, too, for a company our size. As always, the lawyers did well out of it. Getting the good news was probably one of the biggest moments of relief I have experienced in business. I ran around the car park outside the office with my hands above my head shouting like a madman.

Doing the deal with Amazon involved lots of toing and froing between us. But like the earlier LOVEFiLM and Video Island merger, the deal made so much sense for both sides. It gave us the critical mass we needed. With a seat on our board they effectively became part of the business. Crucially we got critical mass in Germany for the first time.

ORGANIC GROWTH AND ACQUISITIONS

"While sealing the big deal is very exciting and motivating don't underestimate the integration requirements afterwards."

It was a big job to migrate the Amazon customers to the LOVEFiLM platform but the team did a great job. It was hard work, but we actually lost very few customers in the process and I would guess that a lot of those who left were probably customers of both.

In 2008, thanks to this deal the business grew by more than 70%. About 35% of that was organic growth and the other 35% was the Amazon deal. But that indicates an important point. While it's all well and good to focus on these key deals, the rest of the business also needs attention.

And while sealing the big deal is very exciting and motivating and keeping the momentum going in the lead-up to that big moment is all well and good, don't underestimate the integration requirements afterwards. Most deals fail not because it's a bad idea strategically but because you can't bring people with you or make the two businesses work together.

When we completed the Amazon deal we didn't need any extra people at the head office level to get the deal completed and the business integrated. We needed a few extra at the direct cost level because we had more customers, but we didn't add a single indirect person. On the upside, other firms stopped sniffing about the business for the time being. A lot of people thought that now that Amazon was on the board we would inevitably end up as part of Amazon. We were less certain at that stage that it would happen that way. Amazon had a lot of belief in the business and brought a very positive attitude and cash and customers into the business, which allowed us to keep on growing at an accelerating rate.

MAKING A DIGITAL MOVE

It was in 2008 that we began to get some clarity in terms of what was happening in the digital market segment. As a result I took the decision to hire a special digital team and set them up as a focused, separate team within the organization. I did this because although it was early days and digital was still very small, we knew it would be huge for the future of the business. But while we knew it was important, I figured it would be hard for everyone in the existing team to give up, say, 10% of their time to do something that didn't impact on the day-to-day business. We created a new organizational structure that allowed for a digital team to focus on getting that product working, get it all moving and give that new side of the business the momentum it needed; only several years later, after the full Amazon acquisition, did that get rolled back into the main organization.

From the customers' perspective nothing changed much. This is a vital lesson for all businesses. What matters to you as a business and what makes sense in terms of organizational structure isn't of interest to customers in itself. They want the same quality of service and, wherever possible, we opted to give them added value for no extra cost.

As with Blu-ray, the digital service, when it came on-stream, was extra value for no extra charge. To build that digital team we went into the market and cherry-picked stars from existing industry leaders. In 2008, this meant the BBC and of course Sky.

We had seen that we would have to offer a digital service as early as 2005. At that time it wasn't clear which way the market would go (in terms of downloads streaming) and so we used technology provided by one of our shareholder companies. The problem was it didn't work. Nearly a third of all downloads were ending up with customers complaining, which is clearly not a scalable model.

SWITCHING HORSES MID-RACE

So we pulled out and stopped offering it. We basically withdrew from the whole digital segment for a while, in order to gather our thoughts and look at where the industry was moving. What was obvious was that with the emergence of a decent high-speed broadband network and the launch of the BBC's iPlayer, the whole industry was moving towards streaming.

We had backed downloads, probably in part because it was the closest digital equivalent to our physical rental business. We therefore had to switch horses mid-race and that naturally put us behind the market a bit. The senior team were right behind me on this but the only way I could see of regaining that ground was to have a group of the very best people with a single-minded determination and focus on digital.

So we headed for the BBC and hired Ben Lavender, who helped design, build and develop the iPlayer, and Mark Hewis, a platform engineer. We also managed to hire, first of all as a consultant and then full time to lead the group, Lesley McKenzie, an ex-Sky employee who had done a significant number of deals on content acquisition for film and TV. These, along with many others, were the best and most experienced talent from across the industry and we had to pay significant amounts to get them, especially as we had no service to launch at that time.

TAPPING THE FINANCIAL MARKETS AS A CRISIS LOOMS

This investment in the digital side of the business cost money and it was in 2008 that we decided to go back to the market to talk to investors. All sorts of deals were on the table, including a potential Initial Public Offering (IPO), or flotation. The trouble was that without a clear digital offering we went to market without the full story. It was half a story at best. And, despite the best efforts of the advisors, who were appointed on a contingency fee basis – which meant they only made any money if they managed to help secure a deal – this was our least successful visit to the market.

It didn't help that it was late 2008 and we were out in the market seeking funds just as Lehman Brothers collapsed. We were literally presenting to people who had stopped listening to us and were all looking at their BlackBerrys, watching portfolios plummet. To be honest it was obvious that our story didn't stack up and the market wasn't in the mood. It pretty much shut down at that time. But because we were working with corporate finance advisors on a contingency fee basis, they kept us out trawling round the market longer than we should have been.

There is a time when you need to recognize it's not going to happen and pack up and go home. By staying out there so long we looked desperate and it didn't do our brand or reputation any good. In fact I think it damaged us a bit.

Around that time there were also lots of leaks to the business press. So there would be big front-page stories in the *Sunday Times* about how LOVEFiLM was up for sale and how the founders were all going to make tens of millions of pounds. Most of it was inaccurate rubbish, leaked, it would seem, by the advisors to keep the story alive and get someone interested. It really didn't help and caused a lot of annoyance and uncertainty within the business.

Lessons from Partnership

1. **Leaders must be firm as well as fair.** While effective leaders need to be aware of the softer people skills and be emotionally engaged, it's also important to be seen to be decisive and to act quickly.
2. **Be wary of big businesses expressing an interest in buying some or all of your business.** They won't value your time as much as you do and they often turn out to be wasting time.
3. **Listen to all serious offers, and be polite but resolute.** Do what you can to learn about them. Discovering how you fit with their plans may help your strategy.
4. **Make sure you are in the room with the right people.** Don't settle for anyone less than the key decision maker.
5. **Keep all conversations open and moving.** It's very difficult to predict which ones will pay off and which ones will go nowhere.
6. **Don't forget to prepare for life after the deal.** While sealing a big deal is exciting and motivating, make sure you make the effort to integrate organizations fully.
7. **Don't think customers care about things just because you do.** What matters in terms of organizational structure, for example, isn't of interest to customers.

CHAPTER 9
2009: GROUNDHOG DAY

Why there's no substitute for hard graft

Groundhog Day

Released: 1993

Director: Harold Ramis

Cast: Bill Murray, Andie MacDowell

Synopsis: An egocentric TV weatherman who, during a hated assignment covering the annual Groundhog Day event in Punxsutawney, finds himself repeating the same day over and over again.

Awards: 1 BAFTA (Screenplay)

Trivia: Bill Murray was bitten by the groundhog twice during shooting. Director Harold Ramis originally wanted Tom Hanks for the lead role, but decided against it, saying that Hanks was "too nice".

By any measures, 2009 was a terrible year for the global economy. The shock of the 2008 financial collapse sent the world's economy into what has become known as the great recession, although it wasn't that great for a lot of people and a lot of businesses. But businesses don't all suffer equally in a recession and it's fair to say that LOVE-FiLM was one of the luckier businesses.

For LOVEFiLM 2009 was all about consolidation and the hard daily grind of running a business. It's why I think *Groundhog Day* is a great choice for the film for this year. We had integrated the Amazon customers into the business quickly and with very little pain in terms of lost consumers. That happened because, as I describe later, we had the right performance review and management systems in place. The systems were all in place for us to grow and keep taking on more customers. One early insight we had had was that our highest growth rate was in postcodes where we had the greatest penetration. This had proved the extent to which LOVEFiLM was a business that was all about word of mouth and referral. So alongside all the elements you'd expect in a traditional marketing mix, we also invested quite a lot in member-get-member referral marketing.

"Many VCs and entrepreneurs find that, once the thrill and magic of the start-up is gone, the reality of the daily grind of delivery and execution is simply beyond their expertise or interest."

Customers as Marketers

Getting your own customers to help you market your service is one of the most effective things you can do. But to make this work you need to do a few things well. First, you need a service that delivers such great value and works so well that customers will want to talk about it. When we started off in DVD rental we were about 50% of the cost of a high street rental and typically had 10 to 20 times the choice they did. We therefore had a clear advantage. However, it was not until 2007, when we launched our TV campaign, that we began to get the word of mouth moving and working for us. As the loyalty built, and importantly customers felt they had discovered something special, which is what we tried to make it, when then we offered vouchers for them to pass on to friends and family, and they were very happy to do this. In the end as our systems developed we were also able to offer them discounts on the service to thank them for referring their friends.

That sort of scheme was how we were able to keep growing during a recession. We were an affordable luxury. More people staying in meant good news for us. But this wasn't an approach that would lead to stellar or spectacular growth. It was, as I've said, a hard daily slog. For many VCs and entrepreneurs this stage is the point when the magic starts to fade. The thrill of start-up was gone and many entrepreneurs find the reality of the daily grind of delivery and execution simply beyond their expertise or interest. This is fair enough, but many entrepreneurs fail to notice that the light has gone out. And fewer still recognize the need to draft in people with the right skills and expertise to run a business day in, day out.

REACHING THE GROWTH TIPPING POINT

There comes a tipping point in every business when you move from being a collection of passionate people just muddling through, to being an organization that requires structure and order and where you have to divide functions more carefully. That is often a difficult time for founders because they move from making all decisions and being involved in everything to making part of a decision and being involved in some areas and not others. They might well find they disagree with decisions made elsewhere in the business. That becomes an interesting inflexion point. Founders often leave or bring in hired help in order to keep the business moving, but more common is that they fail to see the problems building until it is too late.

In truth there are lots of organizations where founders are struggling to cope with that change of business model and who takes on what decisions and what role. But then other founders do a great job of finding the right mentor who can teach and pass on those skills and they are able to keep managing the business through thick and thin. And for its worth, my personal opinion is that if you can find a clear role for the founder to do in a business (and they are happy with that role) then it is good to keep them. No one will ever understand the business like they do and no one has their passion for it. However, if they can't cope with the change going on around them and they still want to make every decision, then you will never be able to scale the business quickly enough and you need to part company. As always, it's best to do this amicably.

Without wishing to sound arrogant, I think LOVEFiLM was lucky in that there were so many founders and funders involved early on that it had recognized the benefit of hiring in great people early on to take over the running of the business. People like Simon Morris, Andrew Ground, Fern O'Sullivan and Jim Buckle all brought with them vast experience of working at senior levels in large organizations. As well as bringing deep consumer insight and analysis, they knew how to keeping an organization running smoothly.

THE ENTREPRENEUR'S SELL-BY DATE

The attitudes and skills that make entrepreneurs good at what they do often don't translate into running an organization. Business success is more about perspiration than inspiration. And as recession really hit home in 2009, it became clear that having assimilated all the Amazon customers, it was time to knuckle down and get on with the day-to-day business of business. We had been out in the City trying to raise funds to help speed up growth even more when Lehman

Brothers collapsed. We didn't succeed and now it was clearly time to just get on with reliving *Groundhog Day*, day after day.

In fact the business was, as I said, relatively immune from the worst aspects of the recession. As consumers' confidence in the future dropped to all-time lows, many businesses struggled and people were either put on short-time working, lost their jobs all together or were worried about these things happening to them. As the phrase of the day would have it, "staying in became the new going out". We were part of a movement of recession-friendly businesses offering affordable entertainment at home. Many supermarkets launched luxury dining at home ranges. Rather than splashing out on visiting the cinema and spending money on expensive food and drink in restaurants, consumers seemed to be staying in with a good movie and high-quality supermarket food. Just as the supermarkets saw sales increase, so we saw subscriptions rise. We were also at this time playing around with different subscription packages. With the retail price of DVDs dropping all the time, we had started to offer capped packages with an entry point below £5 a month. In the same way that supermarkets tried to stretch their offerings to cater for both the premium market (affordable luxuries) and the basic essentials, so we had a wide range of packages to appeal to all types of consumer.

THE POWER OF PERFORMANCE MANAGEMENT

One thing that had always helped LOVEFiLM respond quickly to what was happening in the world and in the industry was its performance review and management system. If you have annual goals it's hard to change goals mid-stream. But we had a quarterly performance review cycle we called Performance Related Pay (PRP) which meant everyone in the business sat down with their manager on a 13-week cycle and reviewed what they'd done.

We also paid people variable pay based not on the performance of the company or their team, but specifically on their own performance that quarter. It was very immediate feedback for everyone and allowed me as CEO to pull together a report every quarter of high achievers and poor performers and the issues, opportunities and challenges facing the business. It was intensive in terms of management time, because everyone was reviewing their entire team and being reviewed every quarter. But that list of organization performance and identifying high performers really helped. Every month I and members of the executive team would take out the high performers for a lunch, often long and boozy. During this lunch we would ask them directly what made them a high performer and how we could all learn from what they did in the last quarter. I think many enjoyed the lunch but I guess the real reward was being selected ahead of their peers as one of the high performers.

That detailed process was fantastic when we were looking at how we were bringing people together to focus on integrating the Amazon customers. It allowed us to really focus everyone. Some people had to change their roles quickly to respond to the pressure on the business and it worked in our favour that we were meeting people so frequently. We didn't need to wait until the end of the year to hold performance reviews. Because we were growing so quickly and changing so much it was really useful to be able to steer the ship with that degree of sensitivity and not have to wait until next year's objectives to set new goals for the teams. It also gave us an advantage because most of our larger competitors were doing it on an annual basis. They don't want their managers sitting down every quarter doing performance reviews.

"Thanks to the review process, managers at LOVEFiLM were encouraged, allowed and expected to do what too many managers don't do. In other words they were actually managing."

As much as I would love to take credit for this approach, it was something that was already in the business when I joined. So it had been put in place very early on, as part of that inherent desire to have as much information on products, customers and people. It was an information-rich organization right from the earliest days.

Sales people are often used to working to quarterly targets and when I was at Dell everyone had quarterly targets. At LOVEFiLM, as things grew and speeded up, it became more and more important. In fact it helped us save money in some ways because we managed to grow to over 300 people before we hired our first HR person. That was because, thanks to the review process, managers were actually managing. They were encouraged, allowed and expected to do what too many managers don't do. In other words they knew what was going on in their teams and could act if something bad was happening. And they were able to encourage more of the good stuff. The key thing was that this was in the culture and the DNA of the business right from the very start. This gets back to the idea of getting to know the rhythm of the business and the key metrics and data you want out of a business.

What this system allows you to do is track people and monitor high performers and poor performers. It means you have a bank of data to refer to and build conversations around and it forces managers to address performance issues in their team quickly and immediately. In annual appraisals you have to try to remember what happened over a year ago. No one can remember the details of the issues from that far back, everything fades over time and you end up having a lot of extra emphasis on recent events. It effectively becomes a review of what's happened in the last quarter.

For some reason people shy away from detailed people management. No one likes having tough conversations with people, but if it is part of the culture from the start people get used to it. In a retail environment, whether it's a supermarket or a coffee shop, you get a daily feedback on what's good and bad performance. When there is less direct feedback it is often harder to see what's really happening and that's where quarterly reviews are really useful.

From a company perspective we would also put out what Tom Peters calls "big hairy audacious goals" (we just called them big goals) and whenever we hit one we would pay everyone a quarter's PRP bonus. So quarterly PRP became a sort of currency within the business.

How to Do PRP Properly

There are myriad ways to structure performance reviews and appraisals. I have worked for several very large organizations and many of them don't get it right. Without question the system we used at LOVEFiLM remains the best system I have encountered. It really allowed the senior management team to have a detailed grasp of what was happening in the business at all times. The individual performance review gave employees a score between 75 and 125. A score of 100 meant that someone was meeting expectations and targets. If you look at someone earning £50,000 a year, £40,000 was basic and £10,000 was PRP. If every quarter they hit 110, then by the end of the year they would have been paid an extra 10% of their variable pay (in this instance £1,000). But the money was payable each quarter. Then when they hit a big goal, they would get an extra £2,750 (the quarterly PRP).

GETTING DIGITAL RIGHT

In 2009 we started to get some really powerful results from our investment in the digital team under the leadership of Lesley McKenzie. They had pulled together an excellent streaming package and we started to build that into the various subscription packages as a free, or "added value", service as we liked to call it. It was now entirely built around the streaming rather than downloads and we started to get decent take-up fairly quickly, although it still represented a tiny fraction of the total business by customers, revenue and all the other measures.

We made sure that, as with all parts of the business, we used all the data and information we could extract to gain better customer insights and improve the service in this way. Indeed an essential part of this period of grinding out the daily efficiencies when you are in this growth and running the business phase is the constant metrics management and taking stock of where you are. It is all about grinding efficiencies, it becomes quite difficult to squeeze more and more efficiency savings out of everything and everyone, but if you are measuring the right things in the right ways at the right time for the rhythm of your business it should be possible to make sure you quickly stop doing stuff that's inefficient and constantly keep doing more of the good stuff. That means managing the finances, stock, people and the marketing activities and product development.

For this approach to work everything right across the business has to be run with the same eye on efficiency. Some people question the wisdom of collecting so much data. To my mind there is a very simple distinction between data and information that helps clear up whether you are measuring and collecting the right stuff. Ask yourself whether you use the information to make sure you are making the right decisions and doing the right things in the right way at the right time for the right people. If you aren't looking at or using the information week to week or day to day and acting on it, then, as was mentioned earlier, the chances are you have data and not information, and you need to go right back to the starting point and think about what information you need to be able to make effective decisions. The cardinal sin, in my book, is to turn up week after week saying that the data isn't right. If you own the metric it's your decision to fix it and make it usable.

Of course it is never easy to get everything right from the start. You don't know what you don't know when you launch a business and as it grows in size and complexity you need to be able to react and change the things you collect. But if you are launching a new business, at least think about what you might need and want to know as the business grows. You should spend at least a day or so early on considering what you need and how to collect it. That allows you to put the systems in place to collect it right from the start.

"Data can be addictive and can paralyze a company. In large organizations, especially, there will be people waiting for perfect data to support any decision and it's rare you ever get that data."

In the modern world, there is always a danger of data overload. If you get too much data you start to lose information. The problem is that it is very difficult to stop and almost impossible to spot until it's too late and you are looking back with hindsight. But as I say, if you are spending all your time looking at figures and not actually making many decisions or taking actions based on it then the chances are you've got data and not information.

However, data can be addictive and can also paralyze you as a company. In large organizations, especially, there will be people who are waiting for perfect data to support any decision and it's rare ever to have perfect data. What happens in this situation is that you can get obsessed with getting everything right to two decimal places and it will never happen. Then you end up waiting a long time and do not make a decision at the time that you should. Sometimes in companies this analysis can be used to avoid making any decision and by the time you have the information it is all too late. Don't let the tyranny of excellence get in the way of good.

Lessons from an Established but Growing Business

1. **Growth can be a grind.** While the early years in business are about excitement and change, to achieve lasting growth you need to get down to the grind of day-to-day business. It can seem boring, but the hard slog is worth it in the end.
2. **Fast growth means growing up.** There comes a tipping point when you move from being a collection of passionate people just muddling through, to being an organization with structure and order. You have to act to create that structure.
3. **Not all entrepreneurs are good at running a mature business.** You may need a different leadership team as the business grows up. Keep the founder involved as long as it makes sense but make sure everyone knows the strengths and weaknesses they bring to the table.
4. **You never get everything right first time, but you must ensure you do stuff and constantly change.** Be on the lookout for when things are wrong and be prepared to change course. Constantly adapt to get to perfection rather than wait for it before doing anything, but be prepared to have to work to achieve it.
5. **Allow and encourage managers to manage.** Insist on instigating a decent performance management process, it will allow your managers to understand what is happening in their teams and help them make decisions accordingly. Publically recognize the high performers, make them feel special.
6. **Set big, audacious goals and let all staff know what they are.** Then make sure you celebrate and reward everyone when you achieve them.
7. **Data can be addictive and can paralyze you.** Don't let the wait for perfect data stifle growth or innovation. But set out knowing the key metrics and information you need to run the business well and grow it quickly.

CHAPTER 10

2010: SLEEPLESS IN SEATTLE

How to make sure you get what you want from a deal

Sleepless in Seattle

Released: 1993

Director: Nora Ephron

Cast: Tom Hanks, Meg Ryan

Synopsis: A recently widowed man's son calls a radio talk show in an attempt to find his father a new partner.

Awards: 2 Oscar nominations (Screenplay, Song)

Trivia: This was the second of three films that Tom Hanks and Meg Ryan had made together.

At times when I think about the LOVEFiLM adventure it seems the plot could have been cooked up in Hollywood. Like the blockbusters we shipped out by the tens of thousands, the events at LOVEFiLM seemed to tick all the boxes for the perfect, modern, corporate drama. In a short time span we had experienced mergers, OFT investigations, fires and advertising triumphs. What scriptwriters call the story arc had been almost too good to be believable. The climax of that story was to be the sale of the business. The VCs would finally get the payoff for their time, loyalty, efforts and investments.

For me the whole Amazon deal exemplifies why you should never try to pre-empt the future. And why you should always be open to meet with all sorts of people whenever you can. I had first made contact with Amazon right back in 2005. I hadn't been in the business very long, and was in the United States to meet with Netflix founder Reed Hastings. On that trip I stopped off in Seattle to meet with some people at Amazon.

We kept in touch and three years later, in 2008, we did the deal that saw them enter the business as minority shareholders, with a seat on the board. From that time on Amazon was committed to doing whatever it could to help the business succeed. It invested a great deal of time, energy and commitment. And yet it was still far from certain that it would eventually buy the remaining shares and take LOVE-FiLM over and make it part of Amazon.

At the end of 2008 one of the VCs on the board was looking to sell some shares. He had a portfolio that had, by its nature, been badly hit by the recession. He wanted to sell his LOVEFiLM stake and approached Amazon about them buying it. To be honest I think that annoyed some of the other investors, because they felt it gave Amazon a more powerful position, but that's the nature of life with several VCs on the same board. Getting them all aligned and wanting to do the same thing at the same time is tough.

ALWAYS LOOKING FOR THE EXIT

VCs' attitudes to selling something in their portfolio depend partly on the situation in that business but can also have more to do with what's going on elsewhere in their portfolio. If they have just managed to sell something for a huge sum and have plenty of cash in the fund, then they are likely to be in favour of waiting and growing more value before exit for their other companies. But if they haven't sold anything for a while they will be much more likely to want to sell.

Amazon took up that extra stock and I think that likely triggered a whole discussion internally about the role of LOVEFiLM within their business and what they were going to do with us. They were keen to get more shares, partly because around this time we were really accelerating our digital proposition and the new team was performing very well. We were getting a decent number of weekly views and digital subscribers and all of a sudden that transformed the business. We were no longer a physical-only player. We were a hybrid physical and digital player and Amazon clearly wanted a digital content business in Europe.

What happened is that during the process they went through for the internal sign-off to buy the first extra tranche of shares – and being a public organization they have very rigorous internal sign-off processes – they started to discuss buying the rest.

I obviously wasn't party to that discussion, but I imagine it would have covered when – having initially bought some of LOVEFiLM and given that the digital business was going so well and that the business was therefore only likely to get more valuable over time – it would be the right time for them to buy up the rest of the shares. And they seemed to decide that sooner made more sense than later, because it led directly to them enquiring if it would be possible to acquire the bit of the company they didn't own, which was most of it. That was mid-2010 and it took the best part of nine months to get it right and make it happen.

IS THERE A RIGHT TIME TO SELL?

Internally at LOVEFiLM our minds were focused on whether now was the time to sell. We had always grown quickly thanks in part to

*"It became
obvious to the
board that a
strategic partner
with deep
pockets was
going to be a
better long-term
option than being
subject to the
vagaries and
volatility of the
markets."*

having raised plenty of money, but we were now competing with the entertainment giants like Sky and Virgin Media – and Netflix looked like it was soon to come back to the UK. To survive and thrive, LOVEFiLM needed deep pockets to invest in new products, digital film and TV content to constantly improve the experience for existing customers and to spend on marketing to try to recruit more. It's fair to say the mood to sell was gathering momentum.

There had been a lot of speculation in the press since 2008, and occasionally before that, that we were looking at floating the company. In fact we appointed Goldman Sachs way back in 2006 to advise us on the best way to do that. Being a public company requires you to have a good consistent track record of profit and delivery and requires strong and stable business and management. As competitors such as Sky and Virgin were becoming larger companies we would clearly need to be of a certain size if we were going to compete and go public as both of them were. The challenge was that just as we were reaching a credible size the market imploded as a result of the financial crisis and was shut to new IPOs. We were constantly looking at the right time for an exit and at all the options including an IPO. But it was becoming clear that as the cost of digital content was increasing we would need both deep pockets and to raise a lot of money on public markets to get what we needed from the financial markets. For example, it would have been very difficult to raise double our market value to speculatively invest in digital content hoping for our customer base to take off. So it became more obvious to me and to the board that a strategic partner of scale with deep pockets was going to be a better long-term option than being subject to the vagaries and volatility of the markets trying to raise money for a digital business that was still in its very early stages.

None of the existing VCs was in a position to take it over themselves. They were mostly early stage funds and the only other option would have been a private equity deal, but that was complicated by the fact that we had this huge strategic shareholder called Amazon. That made it a very unattractive deal for private equity backers because it wouldn't be a clean deal where they had the controlling stake.

Selling the Company

Important lessons to remember when you are looking to sell a business:

1. **Identify potential buyers as early as possible.** I spotted Amazon as a potential partner in 2005. Having identified them, build relationships and keep a dialogue going. You don't know where you will find the future buyer. We looked all over the place and then found the diamonds in our own back yard and a buyer on our board.
2. **Collect together the proof points that make your business interesting.** We had facts and figures such as 80% of customers who left the business would recommend it to others and that our fastest growth rate was in postcode areas in which we had greatest penetration. Those bits of data are important signs of the firm's potential.
3. **Be prepared for the deal to be more difficult than you expect** and recognize that it may take a lot of diplomacy to align interested parties. It always takes a lot longer than you would like to get through the process and the legal agreements to get to the position to do a deal.
4. **Be selective in who you share what information with internally.** You don't want to distract too many people away from the day-to-day running of the business, especially because it can take months to be completed.

WHAT'S THE BIG DEAL?

This deal was a big deal for both parties and it was natural that both sides would want to do what's called due diligence. This is particularly relevant for the buyer, who is parting with cash and wants to make as sure as they possibly can that they are buying what they think they are and that they are getting good value for their own shareholders.

Whenever you do due diligence, make sure you keep a record of all your documents. This is the time when, if you've planned for the start of a sale, you get to use information you've collected together about the business to prove its value. With plug-in hard drives, there is no excuse these days for not getting right into the detail of the business. And having everything in place.

As you'd expect, Amazon was extremely diligent about looking right through all our finances and it interviewed a lot of people. When you do due diligence you set up what's called a data room. That used to be a physical room where documents could be securely stored and looked at by either party. Now it is more likely to be a shared drive or folder on a drive where documents are uploaded as needed. The beauty of this is that it's obvious who is looking at what files and when. I can tell you that Amazon looked at all the files. From the LOVEFiLM side, as well as the board, the only people who knew about the potential sale were our legal head David Martin, the CFO Jim Buckle and me. That circle widened as the deal progressed and more people got involved and we had to get people to sign confidentiality agreements to ensure it all stayed as quiet as possible.

But despite this, the deal with Amazon wasn't necessarily a done deal or a certainty to go ahead. The big issue for the investors was always creating maximum value and that was the one thing they were all aligned behind, the idea of extracting maximum value from any sale. As the man in the middle, trying to make the deal happen, it was often tricky.

I was discussing certain aspects of the deal to Amazon and other parts to the internal board. The trick in these situations is to recognize that there is no perfect deal that will make everyone 100% happy. At the same time, while I was being realistic about what had to happen to get the deal done, I also recognized that our shareholders had been with us from the start, had been very supportive over many years and we therefore had a certain duty to them.

Needless to say there were more than a few fraught discussions during 2010 and even into 2011. I saw that as a positive thing because it was a sign that there were lots of people who were very passionate about the business.

During 2010, the Amazon deal was taking up plenty of time and energy. The Amazon team, based in Seattle, were also putting huge amounts of time and resource into it. They were flying out to the UK a lot and were staying up late or getting up in the middle of the night to hold telephone conference calls and meetings with us. That's why this year is about *Sleepless in Seattle*. For our part, as well as doing the deal, we were busy getting the digital platform and plan up and working really well. In discussion with Amazon it became clear that no one else had their platform working as well as we did at that time. That made us a very attractive proposition for Amazon.

JOLLY HOCKEY STICKS

As much as this was good news for Amazon, it was also difficult for the VCs because they could see the business on the verge of really taking off online. The party was about to stop just as it had really got going. But you have to also be realistic. The grass is always greener in the future. As you look at a business plan on a spreadsheet, you can always see the business about to boom into the future, this is often euphemistically referred to as the "hockey stick" principle, i.e. it's always rosy in the future. The truth

"Picking the right advisors is possibly the single most important thing to get right when you're selling a business, or indeed doing any deal."

is that there are execution risks, competitive risks and other unknown risks that the business is going to have to overcome. So people could see that it made sense to sell to the right partner now.

One of the key things in getting any deal through is the role that non-executive directors, independent directors and friendly independent advisors play. It's important as the person driving a deal through that you recognize that a lot of people have vested interests. You always have to try to see behind someone's advice to understand their perspective and why they would make any suggestions they are proposing. And it goes without saying that finding the right lawyers and other advisors is also essential. In fact, picking the right advisors is possibly the single most important thing to get right when you're selling a business, or indeed doing any deal.

Recommendations from other people are always useful, but it's about getting to know and trust the people advising you. Ultimately, you have to be able to know that if you were in the trenches alongside them you could and would trust them and know they are on your side.

For me this is where our chairman Charles Gurassa played an important role in holding a line internally and externally. He had been chairman since just after the Video Island and LOVEFiLM merger in 2006. That meant he knew our story and culture and the personalities involved, but he was also independent in that he was not an investor representative.

Charles was helpful in that the role he played allowed me also to keep an eye on running the business, which in 2010 was increasingly about getting the big digital calls right. The whole digital world had exploded since the BBC's iPlayer had launched. We were busy getting our streaming service launched on as many devices as possible. We took a call that while we wanted to go to a streaming service, we didn't want to clutter up customers' sitting rooms with yet another set-top box or device. So our strategy was to launch the service on existing bits of household kit. That meant long and complex discussions with the makers of those pieces of kit, as well as new deals with the studios.

We went live with the Sony PS3 platform, which was a huge launch and a totally innovative approach for the industry. We also launched on Samsung Internet-enabled TVs and Sony Bravia TVs. And we began to do a full digital over-the-top service. It was a huge amount of work for the digital team, but in 2010 I think it began to pay off for everybody. We also worked with a company to help us with technology in this area. It was called Push Button and founded by two wizards, Paula Byrne and James Cumberbatch. Given its strength and skills in this area it was also eventually acquired by Amazon in 2011.

All this started to build momentum. We hired some really great talent and got things moving very quickly. One example of this paying off was getting through the Sony technical approval process to be on the Bravia. It was the first time that this approval had ever been given first time with no issues; all other third parties were rejected during that process. That was a real credit to the team. We started launching innovative new products in the market place on an almost monthly basis. All of them were presented as added value and part of the original subscriptions. Our strategy was a simple one, to allow as many people as possible in as many ways as possible to access LOVE-FiLM content. The easier we made it to stream and watch our films the more films they would watch. It was good for them, good for us and good for the studios and content owners. Again everyone was winning from it, which is why everyone seemed to support it.

This experience was typical of the technology industry. The time it takes to get something off the ground is always longer than expected, but once you get it out things happen much more quickly than you expect. With the launch of Netflix in the UK and the new Sky Movies service, the industry is moving and growing a lot more quickly than anyone thought it would do. That is partly down to that "app mentality" which has brought out a philosophy that everything has to be instantly accessible on a lot of devices. As well as mobile devices there are apps for computers and now for TVs, which are providing a lot more access to digital content for people in their homes.

It is indeed difficult to do justice to the real intensity and pressure of the digital development team and the incredible way that team pulled together to produce huge new and innovative developments in such short timescales. Following this we then looked at the structure and approach of all our marketing and communications activity to make sure that we had brought the digital and physical offerings together. Later on we also started to offer a digital-only package for those customers who were no longer interested in physical product; many of them no longer owned a standalone DVD player, unthinkable just a couple of years previously.

All of this has meant that we had to go through some major cultural changes. Because while the digital team got a lot of attention and support from the senior team, we also needed to keep the people in the traditional side of the business happy and engaged, not only with their own work, but also with what the digital side of the business was doing, even if they weren't directly involved. They needed to be reminded that the business was still predominantly physical and that even at this time, in 2012, our physical DVD rental business was still growing and the number of rentals every week was still at record levels.

Lessons from the Big Deal

1. **Business is unpredictable.** Don't try to prejudge the outcome of a situation in business. Especially in a fast-growth business and a dynamic industry, almost anything can happen.

2. **Keep your options open.** Because anything might happen you never know which meetings might turn out to be significant. Don't turn down an opportunity to meet someone interesting, because something interesting might come from it.

3. **All deals take longer than you expect.** You need patience in negotiation. No matter how simple a deal looks, there are always complicating factors to overcome. It will take longer than you thought it would. And it will cost more.

4. **Always negotiate for a win/win.** Trying to score points over someone else usually ends in disaster. Work hard for an outcome that pleases everyone a bit.

5. **Don't let big personalities spoil a deal.** Insist on instigating a decent performance management process, it will allow your managers to understand what is happening in their teams and help them make decisions accordingly.

6. **Pick your advisors and non-executives carefully.** During the run-up to the sale we hired some great non-execs that helped when it came to the sale. We trusted them fully at all times to do what was right for us. As you've spent time and money hiring them, listen carefully to their advice when they offer it.

7. **Predicting technology can be tough.** Be prepared to get it wrong. Don't stubbornly stick to a path if the industry data and intelligence suggests you are wrong.

CHAPTER 11
2011: JERRY MAGUIRE

How much work it takes before you see the money

Jerry Maguire

Released: 1996

Director: Cameron Crowe

Cast: Tom Cruise, Renée Zellweger, Cuba Gooding Jr

Synopsis: When a sports agent has a moral epiphany and is fired for expressing it, he decides to put his new philosophy to the test as an independent with the only athlete who stays with him.

Awards: 1 Oscar (Supporting Actor)

Trivia: This was Tom Cruise's fifth consecutive $100m-plus film, which was a new record. The main character's memo and mission statement was directly influenced by Jeffrey Katzenberg's tirade after leaving Disney. The two most memorable quotes from the film are "Show me the money" and "You had me at hello".

Can you remember what you were doing and where you were on Thursday 20 January 2011? I doubt many people can. It's not up there in the pantheon of remarkable news days. It wasn't as shocking as September 11, 2001 or the day President Kennedy was assassinated. But for me – and most other people involved in LOVEFiLM – it was precisely the sort of day that you never forget. This was the day the deal with Amazon was announced.

We'd come to an agreement a few days earlier. There was a sense that we'd all achieved something special for the business. We'd managed to find a strategic partner with deep enough pockets to make sure the business had the money to invest in constantly evolving and developing technologies. We were now on the verge of very exciting times for the business.

"One key lesson from all this is to make sure you and the board are fully aligned behind what it is you want to achieve and what sale value you will say yes and no to."

It is fair to say that there were considerable sensitivities around the conversations that could take place at board level about us finding a buyer and a long-term partner, considering that Amazon had a seat on the board. But we always operated in a spirit of openness and transparency and Amazon was always very committed to helping us achieve what was best for the long-term health of the business. But there were possibly more conversations around the fringes of the main board and there were some difficult decisions to be made about who to include in conversations and phone calls and who to leave out.

It had been a very difficult deal to pull together. Amazon rightly has a reputation for being tough negotiators. I think the final deal will prove a great one for everyone and for all parties, but it took a lot of effort and negotiation for us to get there.

THE IMPORTANCE OF BOARD ALIGNMENT

One key lesson from all this is to make sure you and the board are fully aligned behind what it is you want to achieve and what sale value you will say yes and no to. This is where your non-executive directors can help. For two years in the run-up to the sale, our non-executive chairman Charles Gurassa had strengthened the board with some non-investor directors who could help us at the time of a sale if the company ever went public. These directors were independent and this meant they could consider any deal in isolation of a shareholding. This led to some good debate and ultimately a clear mandate supported by everybody. If there is that total clarity in your mandate for the deal that will and won't be accepted, then you can save time in that you won't be taking back offers that you know will be rejected.

It is also essential that you have key roles and responsibilities for the deal defined by the board and make sure everyone knows what they are doing. Charles played a pivotal role in those discussions and how they were going to work. I have no doubt the process wouldn't have got done without him there brokering the deal on our side and organizing the discussions between the VCs and the non-executive directors. That was his role and he knew that was what he was there to do, so the negotiating team had good authority to get on and do the deal. If you don't have the roles clearly agreed the process can go all over the shop and it starts to get very messy, very quickly. This is the sort of detail that leads many deals to fall apart, even where they would make good strategic sense.

PICKING THE RIGHT ADVISORS

We had some informal external advice but we didn't seek to appoint corporate finance advisors. Generally this would be the best thing to do and picking the right advisors will make the whole experience much easier and a little less stressful. But in this instance the LOVE-FiLM board was stuffed full of investors and deal makers any one of whom probably had more experience than many of the corporate finance advisors. We did have an excellent lawyer heading up our side in Liz Field at Stephenson Harwood.

Although I was keen to get the deal together and even though Amazon was also one of my shareholders, I was clearly more on the side of the LOVEFiLM investors, we had been working together for over seven years for this day and I wanted the best possible price. To be fair, I was also a minority shareholder myself. The challenge was getting alignment on our side. We also had other minority shareholders and had to look into what they needed and make sure they were communicated to properly all through the process.

There were quite a number of these minority shareholders, many of whom were the former founders or employees of the business and towards the end of the negotiation they became quite difficult. They banded together and caused a fuss. We just had to deal with them the way we dealt with everyone, which was fairly and honestly and trying to get them aligned with the deal. With the small investors, the issue was that everyone felt they could do better and they sensed the end was coming. They were all armchair negotiators and everyone had a view on any deal and everyone wanted to get involved in any potential valuation. But they didn't know the Amazon deal that was being negotiated and the challenge was keeping them onside during any deal process. However, to get the deal to happen you need a certain proportion on side. And over 10% of the company was still owned by these minority shareholders.

You think the deal is done and then it takes a lot of finalizing and work to get it the last few hundred metres over the line. It was a real marathon of a deal and while we had the all-clear from the UK competition authorities we had to get approval in Germany which we did.

Then we had to start aligning everyone behind the deal. Once it was signed and approved we could announce it internally. Amazingly, nothing had been leaked about it. Although in the process we had had to extend the group of people who knew and got them to sign confidentiality agreements, the number of those in the know was still quite limited. Eventually we were able to pull everyone together in January and announced the deal.

When we announced the deal at the all-staff meeting we got this massive cheer and a round of applause from all the staff. It was an amazing response and it happened because they really understood the business and recognized what a positive and good home Amazon would be for LOVEFiLM.

It was a very emotional moment. When you've been working so hard for such a long time to secure a deal and as it is announced you get that response from staff, it was amazing. We had some senior Amazon people over from Seattle who saw the staff give them a round of applause and were very excited about the changes that were going to take place. That became a great day for me, for LOVEFiLM and I think also for Amazon.

And before you think it, there was no mention at this time of my leaving the company. So that wasn't what they were cheering. In fact all but one of the senior team agreed to stay on and take us through the transition phase and then into the long-term future.

A CHAMPAGNE MOMENT FOR THE UK?

It's fair to say that the outside world greeted the announcement of the deal with less than the rapturous enthusiasm the staff had shown, but the coverage was pretty good. I think most intelligent observers could see the logic in what we were doing and in truth not that many were really surprised by it. After all we'd been working so closely with Amazon for a while. The general tone of the reporting was that this was a deal that Amazon had done to prevent us from going down the IPO route to ensure that they maintained control of LOVEFiLM at a time when Netflix was about to come marching into Europe. There was some inevitable noise about the fact that while this represented a win for the UK technology sector, it was also a shame to see the company out of British ownership and in the hands of a US technology giant, while

"It was also fair to say that Amazon recognized that if LOVEFiLM was going to grow in the way we all wanted, Amazon would have to invest heavily in the business."

one or two others compared the reported valuation to Netflix, which had recently been valued at over $10bn.

How the Press Viewed the Deal . . .

Reported in the *Guardian* as "Amazon takes full control of LOVE-FiLM" and on the BBC News website as "Amazon buys remaining stake in LOVEFiLM DVD service", the initial reaction across most print and digital media was to report the facts of the deal, or rather to report the facts that were in the public domain and speculate on those that weren't. But there was also an undercurrent of UK tech bashing, with a tone that mocked the low reported price paid by Amazon (never officially confirmed or denied) and the mere fact that this was another UK tech success selling out too soon to a US giant. The *Financial Times* summed this up with a news article that concluded its first paragraph with the view that this was a deal that saw "another leading UK dotcom company sold to an American suitor".

Meanwhile the BBC's technology correspondent Rory Cellan-Jones questioned whether this was really a champagne moment for the UK tech sector at all. Clearly he didn't think it was and in a blog post he compared the rumoured price paid for LOVEFiLM with the $10bn valuation of US rival Netflix a few months earlier. At the very least, he wrote, the deal would raise the age-old question of "why can't we in Britain grow our own world-beating technology businesses?"

I really didn't agree with this last point. The simple fact is that Netflix was operating in a much bigger geography and had something like 10 times the number of subscribers we did. Interestingly this market cap as of today is less than $4bn. It was also fair to say that Amazon recognized that if LOVEFiLM was going to grow in the way we all wanted, Amazon would have to invest heavily in the business.

So what are the vital lessons we learned from selling the business? I guess the first point is that it helps if you start with the end in mind.

As a business loaded with VCs, the eventual sale or another type of exit (such as an IPO) was always on their minds. So we had to make sure we balanced the needs of the business with the needs of the VCs and other investors. I think we managed to get that balance right most of the time, although we possibly held back from investing more in the business in 2009/2010 in order to boost its profitability ahead of any potential sale. It is also essential to pick your partners carefully when you are doing any deal. And if you are looking for any significant investment remember that those investors are likely to want to join the board and get involved in the business. So make sure that they are the sort of people you think you can work with.

OPINIONS ARE LIKE NOSES

Closing the deal with Amazon also confirmed for me the old adage that opinions are like noses. Everyone has a different one and some smell better than others. It is also important that while you are in the middle of any significant deal that you are prepared to let it dominate your life. I took a skiing holiday in January 2011, just as the Amazon deal was coming to a head. It was ridiculous. I would ski down the mountain, take a call and spend the entire chairlift back up talking to someone and then ski back down and do it all again. But keeping up that communication is vital to the success of any deal. You also have to make sure that you respect everyone's view, so long as they are being reasonable. If they are just being bloody minded then there is reason to push back and tell them not to be such a so and so.

Amazon publicly stated at the time the deal was announced that they would have to put as much money into the business after the deal as they spent on the deal itself. And I can confirm that they have been true to that word in terms of investing in content, people and devices in order to build the business and the brand. They are very decisive about what they do and why they are involved with LOVEFiLM. In Jeff Bezos's first shareholder letter after the Amazon flotation he talked about being absolutely focused on the customer and that they would make decisions based on the long term. From what I have seen I think that is very much the case. They are making long-term decisions to ensure LOVEFiLM is in the best position to win the battle into the future.

Because after the acquisition by Amazon we took some positive and aggressive decisions on things such as film and TV content acquisition early on; I think we were in a much stronger position than we would have been.

I think it is entirely fair to say that there isn't a company on the planet that is better at managing growth than Amazon. And everything we have done so far as a small, independent and privately owned company is different to how things would have worked as part of a large public multinational. There was clearly a period of adjustment coming and there were to be some organizational speed-bumps along the way.

GROWING UP AND GETTING ON

"There is no question that it is much better for LOVEFiLM to be within Amazon, but it will always be a different LOVEFiLM from the standalone business."

2011 was all about LOVEFiLM becoming part of that larger organization. We had to recognize that when we were making decisions there were more things to consider.

Also, as a result, at LOVEFiLM we were now making decisions not regionally, but globally. So technology decisions we made would now have to fit with a global strategy and that takes things to a different and more exciting level, and requires different internal sign-off processes and a very different mindset. That's just the way it is. At LOVEFiLM we have maintained the performance review structure and we still both make sure our managers are managing to that detailed level and give out awards to staff based on the key values. But the Amazon investment means we have doubled the size of the technical operation. That means a lot of new blood has joined that has only known this new world and this different way of doing things. There is no question that it is much better for LOVEFiLM to be within Amazon, but it will always be a different LOVEFiLM from the standalone business.

Lessons from After the Deal

1. **A difficult deal can take over your life.** But if you want the best outcome for a short time you might have to let it. The rewards will be there in the end.

2. **Don't expect everyone to see the deal the way you do.** The staff response to the Amazon deal was overwhelmingly positive, but some observers were critical of what they saw as a "sell-out".

3. **Start with the end in mind.** Make sure you understand what a win looks like for both parties before you start negotiating and make sure your entire board is aligned behind what you think is a win.

4. **Understand what investors want at the start.** It is likely that they will want to have a seat on the board and a say in the future running of the business. Don't enter negotiations if you won't settle for that.

5. **Opinions are like noses.** Everyone has one and all of them are different. And some don't smell as good as others. Respect everyone's view, but only if they are being reasonable.

6. **Be prepared for change.** Doing a big deal with a major investor will inevitably change the culture of your own organization. Don't expect to act like a small company when you are part of a much larger one.

7. **Plan your succession early.** Right from the start when hiring my executive team I thought about who could take over if something happened to me. Jim was the obvious successor.

CHAPTER 12
THE LOVEFiLM YEARS
POST-PRODUCTION

My departure from LOVEFiLM was announced on 7 February 2012. But a lot of preparation work had been going on behind the scenes before then. In many ways being a good leader is not dissimilar to a VC, in that you know there will be an exit at some point in the future and you have to do what you can to plan for that exit, without destabilizing the existing team and without allowing the organization to lose momentum. The secret to a smooth transition and a good succession, as with so much in life, lies in effective planning and strong communication.

Simon's LOVEFiLM Departing Blog

After nearly seven amazing years as head of LOVEFiLM, I have decided the time is right to hand over the baton to the next leader. Growing this company has been a fantastic experience and I have had the pleasure of working with a truly talented team, real innovators who introduced a brand new way for millions of movie lovers to enjoy films. They provided our customers a vast selection of over 70,000 DVDs and video games, and, more recently, led the way in streaming great titles through PCs, TVs, Blu-ray players and games consoles.

I cannot name everyone individually but they know who they are. We have achieved great things for our customers and have positioned LOVEFiLM to do even more. I'd like to thank every member of the team, every customer, every investor and every partner for helping us get to this stage of the journey.

Some of the early milestones and speed-bumps along the way included losing most of our DVD stock in a distribution centre fire; important mergers uniting a number of truly great teams, and embarking on our first national TV campaign which paid off greatly. Every twist was interesting and I learnt a great deal along the way. In 2008, we forged a relationship with Amazon, which was to prove the ultimate home, and the best home, for the future of LOVEFiLM. They have been true to their word and continue to invest even more on behalf of customers. We have now over two million members across Europe and are innovating new services on the PC, PS3, Xbox and iPad, to name but a few.

I am now delighted to be handing over to Jim Buckle, who has been part of the leadership team from the early days in 2006 and who knows LOVEFiLM inside out. Jim has led both finance and commercial, and will now lead the whole business. LOVE-FiLM could not be in better hands and I wish Jim and the whole team tremendous success.

Rest assured I will be keeping my subscription and following every single new turn in this fascinating industry and great company. Thank you for making it such a fantastic company to be part of.

Simon Calver, CEO

A NUMBERS GAME

It's becoming more common for chief financial officers to step up and take the top job. In the case of LOVEFiLM Jim Buckle had been our CFO at the time we did the Amazon deal (and had been since the Video Island and LOVEFiLM merger) and then became commercial director after the deal went through as part of the transition process. That meant he had detailed involvement in all the commercial aspects right across the business, had been on the board for a long time and as well as just the financial stuff he knew how the business ran and what made it tick. He was a clear and obvious successor and he led part of the final Amazon deal as well. He had previously been the managing director of a technology company, so he obviously had the skills to lead the organization into its exciting next phase. Some people worry about CFOs being too inward looking to take on the role of CEO, which is very much outward focused. But at LOVEFiLM there had been so many investment rounds and so many discussions with the VC community that the CFO role was always more outward facing.

Jim was very comfortable talking to all sorts of groups of stakeholders and I knew he could do a fantastic job as managing director for however long he stayed in the post. When the time comes for Jim to move on, I am sure he will also handle his succession smoothly with the senior staff at Amazon.

Now that the transition into the Amazon group and how that is going to work had become clearer, it was obvious that there wasn't really a role for a separate CEO. The role changed a bit, which is part of the reason I felt it was right for me to move on. I wanted to go and run my own thing and search for another great business whose customers felt a real passion for the brand.

It was all agreed with Amazon and it happened that the board of another great British retail brand, Mothercare, were looking for a turnaround CEO and I applied for the job along with other candidates. I was very fortunate to get it and was excited about the challenge of using many of the skills and ideas developed during and pre-LOVEFiLM in the retail sector, albeit at a very challenging time.

PLANNING SUCCESSION IS PLANNING SUCCESS

The early identification of a successor is important. I talked with Jim about it and it was clear he was keen to give it a go. But if there isn't a clear or obvious candidate you can test different people out by giving them ultimate responsibility for key projects or different projects and see how they do. You can also nominate someone to be in charge when you go away and then see how many calls you get while you are away. However you make the decision and whoever you choose, it is essential that you communicate that to the organization and take the team with you.

Internally, we had separated the integration with Amazon into two phases. The first and immediate transition was about keeping the business focused on doing the everyday tasks, keeping the lights on so to speak. And second, working out who was going to do what longer term and where and how. If we didn't get the immediate transition right the business could suffer, while we knew that we had time to get the longer-term plan in place. In my mind I always signed up for the transition. I probably hadn't really thought much beyond that but the important thing for me was that the whole senior team signed up to make that transition, apart from one person who was on the verge of leaving to start his own business anyway and used this as a good opportunity to go.

"However you make the decision and whoever you choose as your successor, it is essential that you communicate that to the organization and take the team with you."

The transition went smoothly and the business continued to accelerate throughout 2011. As the business became more core to what Amazon was doing, it became obvious we would become more integrated into the Amazon company than perhaps we might have expected right at the start.

The announcement of my departure coincided with a massive announcement that we were forming a UK development centre for Amazon video worldwide in London. That would be building on a lot of LOVEFiLM and the Push Button technology and bringing all the core digital competencies and skills together in one centre. That new centre was to be one of Amazon's largest development centres outside the US.

THE DAWNING OF A NEW ERA

It was inevitable that as we reached the end of the transition period, a new LOVEFiLM era would be beginning and there was bound to be another series of personnel and structural changes, which is what happened. At the time you do the deal you never know how it will work out and some of those unknowns are unknown to everyone. The really good news for LOVEFiLM is that events since the deal was completed have made it even more critical to Amazon.

But Amazon's ownership inevitably changed the culture of the business, as it was bound to. Many would argue this was for the better now that we were a global, and not just a European, player. At the time we announced the deal we thought there would be less change in the early years but that the businesses would progressively get more integrated over time. But as time went on I think it has become clear to us all that the opportunity for both was even greater than we had first thought and the degree of integration would have to be greater and quicker if both sides were to realize the benefits of being part of one company.

Without wishing to sound trite, one thing that is absolutely clear to me is that the future of LOVEFiLM is in the best possible hands it could be. It's really a case of this particular story having the happiest possible ending.

LESSONS FROM LOVEFiLM

PART THREE

CHAPTER 13
THE ROLE OF TECHNOLOGY

It's clear that technology is becoming more critical to all companies across all sectors of the economy. But there are still some companies for whom it is just that bit more critical and those are businesses that are broadly regarded as technology companies. A company like LOVEFiLM relies heavily on technology in all areas of the business. But it seems logical that it's more critical still for firms such as Google, Apple and Facebook. And yet, the gap is closing and today any fast-growth business will rely to a large extent on getting its technology right.

START WITH THE CUSTOMER

"Before any technology project gets started, someone at Amazon writes the press release for the customer even before they start the development."

Understanding the point of difference in the user experience online is critical. Some great technology companies, such as Joost and Seesaw, never really succeeded in my view (in digital video in their cases), simply because they didn't have a relevant customer proposition. Apple continues to succeed, where others (most recently Nokia) fail, simply because it puts the customer first. Similarly, Amazon is very smart in this way. It bases all of its decisions on the customer. In fact before any technology project gets started, someone at Amazon writes the press release for the customer even before they start the development or the project itself. Once they feel they have that right, they can get going with the project placing that customer release as the brief at the heart of the project.

A SEAMLESS CUSTOMER EXPERIENCE

Delivering a seamless customer experience is essential, even in times of crisis. So when Video Island's distribution centre burnt down (see Chapter 5), we focused 100% of our energy on continuing to meet customer needs. To do this we needed to ask who within our business owned the customer experience. The answer was at that time (and should always be) that everybody does, as long as the leader believes that.

In order to ensure that everybody had clear visibility to the customer issues and metrics we had charts in the LOVEFiLM reception area showing reasons why customers contacted us with issues and which department was responsible. Not only was it important for staff to understand the reasons for customer failures but this meant we showed visitors and suppliers how seriously we took customer issues. As a leader, in my view you have to set behavioural standards and expectations when it comes to customers. To do that you need to reward good things when and where they happen and equally ensure people know when and where they have fallen short of the mark. If you receive individual customer letters, you should ensure they get a reply either from you or from someone on your behalf very quickly.

SCALE FOR SUCCESS

Scaling the business as you grow is critical, and crucially this means keeping up your high standards of customer service. It might be simple to service customers really well when you have a handful. But how will you keep those levels up when you have thousands, tens of thousands, or more? And keeping the customer happy is more important now than ever. As LOVEFiLM got deeper into the digital model, this service became more immediate, more similar to broadcast TV, such as the BBC or ITV.

"Giving customers who had streamed a film on their PS3 £5 credit got us a fantastic response, especially on Twitter and other social networking services."

Sometimes we did not get this right but an example of getting where we did at LOVEFiLM was our reaction to the PlayStation Network (PSN) outage, which meant customers lost service on their Sony PS3 for several weeks. We responded immediately the service went back up, giving all customers who had ever streamed a film on their PS3 £5 credit. This got us a fantastic response from customers, especially on Twitter and the other social networking services. That response was almost immediate and I am sure we gained credibility with customers from that, even though the crisis was not of our making.

NEW PRODUCTS ARE ALWAYS TECHNOLOGY DEPENDENT

Any new product or new service development in the entertainment industry is technology dependent. We had some issues originally at LOVEFiLM with a so-called "black box" approach to developing products. Those developing them worked on their own and sometimes in secret. Often we had over 80 different things to achieve each month, but because these teams were working in isolation, regardless of how they tracked their progress, we didn't know what was likely to have been done by the end of the month. Often priorities would change and teams had to be shuffled about and that made it harder for others to pick up the development work. We actually improved a lot and gained some really useful insight from working with Amazon in 2008 when we migrated their customers over to LOVEFiLM. To make this project work we created so-called "pizza teams", which were multi-functional teams that owned the development paths or roadmaps in their own areas. This transformed our technology delivery, enabled us to parallel process work and keep expertise within each pizza team to help the development. Some great examples of this later within LOVEFiLM were customer service work or the digital development work on devices.

GROWING UP WITH TECHNOLOGY

"Hire the best people you can. And remember that first division people hire first division, but second division people tend to hire third-rate people."

It's never easy to predict what is going to happen in technology. Several very bright people have made complete fools of themselves by trying and failing to second guess the future. But in a fast-growth business, and especially one with technology at its heart, it is essential that you take some time to try to predict the issues that will arise as the company grows and the technology function becomes a much larger beast. As the organization grows it is likely that the importance and complexity of the IT function will increase.

One major issue is how to grow and still keep things fresh and creative. It is easy to get sucked into a massively bureaucratic, tick-box approach and to lose your creativity along the way. One thing we did at LOVEFiLM was hold a "hackathon" where every developer had a day to work completely on their own ideas. Google has excelled on this, offering staff up to a day a week to do this on a regular basis. Gmail is an example of a successful product that emerged from the process. We had some exciting results but we still needed to prioritize resources to ensure we got these to those major breakthrough moments.

Recruiting and maintaining the quality of a team is essential to success. Are you attracting the right calibre of people? Also, looking at the team you have, are you confident you can grow at speed and get to the next level with these people? The old adage about recruiting people better than you is vitally important, but all too often ignored. From my experience first division people hire first division, but second division people tend to hire third-rate people. This matters across all functions, but in particular in technology you need to have the calibre of people to manage the growth, and scale your technology platform. When we created the new digital business team we hired the very best people. In fact we went out and targeted experts at the BBC, ITV and Sky to build a truly world-class digital team.

Growth can be exciting. But in technology getting bigger as a company means you risk raising your head above the parapet. This has its downsides. You need to be prepared for things such as Denial of Service (DoS) attacks. Cyber-terrorism is on the increase and you need to prepare and protect yourself from it as best as you can as you grow. Sony is still suffering from what happened to its PSN service.

IS YOUR BUSINESS MODEL STILL UP TO THE JOB?

One question you need to consider in technology is the best way to change your business model while still delivering an excellent service on the old one. You can't just sweep the past away, or your business will fall over. But equally you can't stand still and ignore the future, or you will die. At LOVEFiLM, there came a time when it was obvious the business was going to rely less on DVDs and be more digitally focused. When we did the business model migration from physical to digital, we created separate business teams to focus on their individual products. Initially we ignored any cannibalization to start with, deciding that a LOVEFiLM customer was a LOVEFiLM customer, regardless of whether they were using the physical or the digital service.

CHAPTER 14

THE ROLE OF PERFORMANCE MANAGEMENT

There has been a lot already written in this book about the importance of metrics, measurement and knowing the critical success factors and the growth accelerators or inhibitors that will determine the future of the business. This chapter looks in more detail at some of the most important performance management issues.

IF IT MOVES, MEASURE IT

Understanding the metrics that drive the business is critical for success. Building a spider of the relationships between the different business factors is a useful way to get started and understand what you need to know more about. At LOVEFiLM, given we were a subscription business, ultimately revenue was dependent upon the number of paying subscribers we had and the average revenue per subscriber, or ARPU (Average Revenue Per User). The total number of subscribers at any one point in time was a combination of our existing subscriber base, plus any net additional subscribers. ARPU, in turn, is driven by the package mix of subscribers and the cost for each type of package.

"Prompt payment is better for the business than late payment. It is part of reputation management and ensures you maintain good relations with the best suppliers, helping you deliver the best service."

When you work this through for revenue and costs in the business, you begin to understand the drivers of your profit and loss. Similarly you can use this to control and measure cash flow, too. Working through this sort of exercise can help you focus on the key metrics (the elements needed to calculate ARPU, for example) and also help you to work out the critical processes that drive those metrics.

Although this is quite simplistic at a top level, it is possible to drill further and further into this sort of data. And the deeper you get into it, the better quality and richer information you can get. One of the metrics we looked at was cash conversion. This is essentially how quickly we could get cash into the business and how slowly could we let it out. And this isn't about dragging our feet paying smaller suppliers. Prompt payment to suppliers is ultimately better for the business than perennial late payment. It is another part of reputation management and it will ensure you maintain good relations with the best suppliers, helping you deliver the best service you can.

But it did lead us to have more promotions where we only paid partners on a "performance basis". This was all agreed and accepted in advance and it meant we got to do the promotion first, see what the results were and then pay them. Customers came in first and paid us, and then after 30 days or so we paid our partners. That really helped our cash flow, and that is critical in the early days of any company but especially where a company is growing very quickly. At LOVE-FiLM we were growing at lightning quick speeds and better control of cash meant we didn't have to raise even more money and therefore didn't have to dilute share ownership any more than was essential (more on that later).

The Business Spiders

In any business, success comes from being able to interpret what is happening very quickly. Even in a small start-up business, where it should be relatively simple to keep on top of what's actually happening in terms of sales and costs, it helps to understand the algorithms and relationships of how the business actually works. For a larger business, where you have less chance of knowing everything that's going on, and where data is your only useful way of getting to know that, understanding these relationships is crucial.

Take the example of a subscription business. Here the aim is always to increase the lifetime value of customers. But you need to know something as simple as the fact that lifetime value is equal to gross margin per month over the churn rate. This means the only way to increase lifetime value is either to increase gross margin per month or decrease churn rate. Gross margin is made

(Continued)

up of costs and revenues and how many products people are using (and there's another algorithm or equation to work out based around that) while churn rate is based on how many people leave and there'll be another algorithm around that. But the whole business is based on what I call a business spider.

If I set the goal as profit rather than cash, then I know that profit is a combination of revenue and costs. I know revenue in subscription businesses is made up of the number of subscribers times the average revenue per user (ARPU). And ARPU in turn is made up of your package mix, so you can begin to build information out of data. At the end of the spider you get to a series of metrics that you need to measure that will tell you ultimately whether you will achieve your goal for profit or not. But much more importantly these metrics will explain why you will or won't achieve that goal and will show you what needs to be improved and where you should dedicate resources to improving things. For a transactional business like sales, the metrics and how they all fit together will be different to a subscription business and that will be different to a service business.

As the owner or a manager in a business it is quite an interesting exercise to sit down and think about this and work out what are the key drivers and algorithms and the data relationships in your business. This in turn feeds perfectly into the business planning process because it means that for the first time you are able to plan on the basis of knowledge, data and facts and not just the usual "finger in the wind, this is what we did last year plus or minus 10%" approach.

This is about making sure that even in uncertain or difficult markets, leaders are able to build some robustness into the planning. For example, if you are making assumptions in the business plan that your churn rate will be x%, this allows you to work out the sensitivities of this measure. As I tested out results or got real data this was fed into the model to build some robustness into my business plan and how that works.

GIVE EVERY METRIC AN OWNER

Once you have established the critical metrics for your business, you need to ensure that every metric has a clear owner. Sometimes in business, if more than two or three people or teams own a metric, in truth nobody really does. It can be useful to align the metrics against your organization chart and see how many different people have a metric against them and see if any metrics have been missed out. If you are certain you know the metrics are right, this can

"Once you have established the critical metrics for your business, you need to ensure that every metric has a clear owner."

be a useful way to help you understand if you have the right organizational structure. We had issues like this in the early LOVEFiLM days. No one individual was responsible for driving traffic to the website and that meant that at the end of the day nobody was really focused on it.

MEASURE PEOPLE AS WELL

It is important to align the frequency with which you review people against their metrics with the needs of the business. If you are in a slow-moving environment, where not a lot happens you may be able to get this to work with annual appraisals. But at LOVEFiLM the truth was we (and the industry we were in) were moving so quickly we had everybody in the organization on a quarterly performance review. This was linked to performance related pay. Typically, this ranged from 10 to 20% of salary and the payout was made each quarter, depending on how the individuals themselves performed against their individual goals. As CEO, it meant I had the benefit of seeing how the whole organization was performing against their goals. I was therefore able to rank everybody on how they did. I had a total grasp of what was happening in all parts of the business and early warning of where controls and performance were dipping. It was a powerful tool for a CEO.

It may surprise some people but we were able to reach over 300 people before we hired our first HR manager. This was because the managers themselves really had to manage their own teams, reviewing performance at least twice every 13 weeks. This worked particularly well when we had to align the whole organization against new initiatives such as integrating a new customer base or company acquisition or upgrading our own website.

TEAM GOALS MATTER, TOO

This quarterly performance management system meant everybody had individual goals, but we also needed to make sure everybody worked well together. As a result we introduced bigger, team goals. Whenever we hit one of these key company milestones – such as reaching two million customers or the company reaching profitability – everybody would receive that quarter's PRP payout again (which meant 10 to 20% of that quarter's salary). Appropriately and unexcitedly we called these "Big Goals" (well, it worked for us) and they became an important focus for teams. In the early days we would often accompany a big goal payout with a party or company-wide event to celebrate together. Celebrating success together, especially as you grow so quickly, reminds you that you are doing well and despite the pressure you put on yourself progress is being made. You can be your harshest critic sometimes. Similarly, make sure you recognize the high performers. It is often not about money but about getting the recognition for a job well done. We used to do this whenever possible, in town hall (all hands) meetings, on posters on the walls and in all internal communication. Never forget those who are setting the standards for others.

CUSTOMER FOCUS HAS TO BE CENTRAL TO MANAGEMENT THINKING

Building customer focus into your management is key. We circulated the top customer issues and successes to all staff every week, so people got quick visibility of what was happening. Also, as a leader, sometimes you need to set the standard. In 2007 we had an issue in the Nordics with customer service as we had grown so quickly with a successful promotion.

That was a painful mistake in that region and we decided we needed to act to prevent a repeat of it anywhere else. Everybody was trying to do the best for the customer in the company but often there were trade-offs that people made in order to improve efficiency or save money. But these things were costing us and so I issued a statement to the whole company that nobody was allowed to make a decision that gave a worst customer experience without first agreeing with me. During the first month I had two requests that we managed to resolve and in the second month one. Then there weren't any more, as people began to realize this was serious and to find their own solutions to problems that did not impact the customer negatively.

CHAPTER 15
THE ROLE OF RECRUITMENT AND CULTURE

I am a big supporter of all the activity that has happened in recent years to promote more diversity in boardrooms and shop floors across the country. The more mixed and diverse a company's population is, the more they are likely to reflect, understand and be able to interpret the needs of the customers. But in truth there are some limits to how effective these initiatives will be. Because no matter how hard you try, in the end most leaders end up recruiting in their own image and creating cultures that reflect their personalities. The company you build, especially when you are building at a very fast pace, will almost inevitably look and feel like you. It will be the sort of company you want to work in, so that makes sense.

INVEST TIME AND ENERGY TO GET THE RIGHT PEOPLE

"In my experience, building your direct team is the most important thing you can ever do as a leader. In the first six months at LOVEFiLM I probably spent over 30% of my time getting the team together."

In the early days of any start-up the last thing you want to do is to spend time in lots of interviews. You want to be out there doing deals, making things happen or you want to be actually running the business. But in my experience, building your direct team is the most important thing you can ever do as a leader. In the first six months at LOVEFiLM I probably spent over 30% of my time getting the team together. I needed a team I knew could work together, had similar values and would stay together. There will always be differences and arguments, just as there is in any other family. In fact, if you recruit people with passion you should expect this. But you have to make sure that these key people have respect for each other as well.

Michael Dell taught me one of the most important lessons in recruitment while I was applying for a job at Dell. He told me that "first division people recruit first division people, but second division people recruit third". That is because people who are not great are rarely confident and so they don't like to get in people they perceive might be better than themselves. That is clearly a recipe for a downward spiral in quality. Therefore always be clear what you want, in terms of the ideal qualities and behaviours, as well as the experiences. Decide on the type of person you are after for the team and then set a very high bar in recruitment. If they aren't better than yourself at what you are hiring them to do then don't hire them. In my experience, it is always easier to ride a forward-going horse than one you have to keep "legging on" all of the time.

THE OTHERS ARE WATCHING

Unless this person is only the second person in the company, the rest of the organization will look at the quality of the people you hire to judge how good you are at your job. If you let your team get away with things that the rest of the organization would not be allowed to do, then you will have lowered the bar on total company performance. It is better to have raw talent with passion that needs directing, than it is to focus on getting the finished article that will not change ways and has the wrong behaviour or attitude.

We all get it wrong with recruitment sometimes. I have got recruitment wrong a number of times, typically because I am desperate to get someone into a role that has already taken time to fill. But when I have got it wrong, as I did in the early days at LOVEFiLM in the Nordic region, then I have put my hand up, admitted it and taken action quickly. Taking action is key. With recruitment and people issues it always seems easier to let things rest for a while to see if it gets better. Even worse people like to believe that their extraordinary coaching skills will turn the situation around. But we are not all Sir Clive Woodward, the coach of the English Rugby World Cup winning team, and problems almost never get better with age. All you are doing is delaying the inevitable. You have to face facts and accept when someone isn't working well in your organization. Usually when you finally make the change, eventually the rest of the organization "looks up" and acknowledges that finally you understand that the rest of the team have been carrying X or Y for too long. If you have poor performers, then don't worry about the rest of the team if you take them

out. They will have known they were underperforming way before
you did.

DEFINING ORGANIZATIONAL CULTURE

*"Don't waste
money on
consultants to
establish your
company's
values, save it
and give it out as
awards to people
you see
displaying
behaviours you
want to
encourage."*

There are many factors at play in the creation and
defining of the culture of an organization. Often
larger companies spend tens of thousands (or even
hundreds of thousands) on consultancies to help
them define values and decide on a vision. But ask
any successful entrepreneur about this and they will
think it is pretty simple. Work with the staff to
determine the things you all see as important, write
them down and do a bit of word-smithing and then
live them. That's all there is to it. How you behave
is so much more important than anything written
on any page. So if you talk about "having respect
for the team" or "empowering people as a company"
and then you badger and bully people (or even
worse you let somebody on your team do it), you might as well tear
up every piece of paper with the values written on it. People take their
cues from what happens every day and not what you say in fancy
town hall meetings or even what is written on the walls (even if it is
written on a fancy blackboard or groovy whiteboard). So don't spend
all that money on consultants, save it and give it out as awards to
people you see displaying the behaviours you want to encourage.

At LOVEFiLM, we had five values (not untypical for this sort of
thing) around the areas of innovation, being an all-star cast, passion,
being famous for the right stuff and, of course, loving our customers.
We used to give awards out at monthly town hall meetings to people
who displayed great behaviours against these values. We also used to
circulate to all staff weekly top customer feedback against the values,
because if you really start to live these values, then customers feel it
as well. One great example of an award was after we had acquired

Amazon's DVD rental service customers and we were looking for ways to take the Amazon labels off DVDs so we could replace them with LOVEFiLM labels. This job took forever and broke many nails and DVDs in the process. Our distribution centre manager, Andrew, was always looking for new ways to do things but this process was defeating him. One night at home he watched his wife use one of those facial steamers and jumped up, took some of these DVDs out of his briefcase (because he took work home with him) and after a brief time over the facial spa the label came off easily with the DVD unscratched. For the next week we were the largest purchaser of facial steamers in the Peterborough area and we got through the hundreds of thousands of DVDs a lot more quickly and easily. This shows that innovation is a cultural thing, it is not a process governed by a few marketers or technologists. Everybody has the opportunity to innovate and naturally Andrew received one of our monthly awards.

My Management Toolkit

There are three parts to the toolkit: how to manage job performance, tips on managing people and ideas on managing yourself and achieving personal success. These are the values I have built my career on and I like to think that as much as they have worked for me, they will also work for you. But management success is also about being true to yourself, so you'll also need to adjust and adapt these values to create your own personal set that reflects who you are as an individual and that you are authentic to your style and personality. Having gone through that process, make sure you regularly test your actions against these values to see how you measure up to your ideal and how true you are being to yourself.

(Continued)

Managing Job Performance

- Every job we do can be broken down into a series of tasks. There is never a shortage of tasks for us to complete. However, successful leaders are the ones who can prioritize the important versus the urgent and can align resources against these to get them completed.
- Make sure you know exactly what you are responsible for and that, in your team, everybody understands what is expected of them. Manage to 30-, 60- and 90-day horizons, update your list weekly if possible but at least monthly.
- DELIVER on large and small tasks. Don't be satisfied with "just hitting" the number, build a personal reputation for delivery and getting things done. People will be promoted and rewarded based on what is done, not on effort put in or quality of plans.
- Speed is critical, learn to synthesize information and turn into quick decision making. Constantly hone your ability to turn data into action; it will differentiate you.

Managing People

- Meetings: ensure there is a clear objective, let people know ahead of time why you are having the meeting and pre-circulate the agenda. Invite only those people who will help you achieve your objective. Don't turn up unprepared.
- Take actions from all meetings and take a leadership role in following up on those actions. Start and finish on time, show respect for each other's time.
- Team dynamics: we need to be one team, become adept at helping resolve conflicts/differences across all functions and businesses. Be easy to work with and help others in their work. I call it becoming the "glue" that binds the teams together not the treacle that slows things down.
- Hire people better than you are, it will make your life easier. Build a strong team and let them at it! Measure team results

on delivery. Reward and recognize performance on what is achieved not on the effort put in.

- Coach: your job is to develop your management talent. Spend time every week in one-on-ones and team feedback sessions to understand how you can do things better, faster or cheaper. Ask people how you perform as a manager, listen to their feedback and take actions to improve.

Managing Yourself

- Be a learner all of the time, become hungry to understand how other teams and products work so that you can work better with them. Invite yourself to lunch with other teams, don't just go with yours all of the time, every time.
- Become a passionate advocate of the company, what we do and all of our brands and products. Make every decision as if it were your own money; it is.
- Do not take part in gossip, speculation or "bad mouthing" other people or functions. Being given confidential information is a privilege, do not abuse it or you will lose it.
- Be ambitious for the business rather than for yourself. Achieving the first will achieve the second. Doing it the right way and bringing others with you is important.
- Don't be defensive. Don't limit the data others see or get. We need to live continuous improvement and that means we all have the right to give input; treat this as helpful.
- Believe in yourself but watch the arrogance. There is a fine line between self-confidence and excessive ego.
- Note, positive energy is infectious; everybody wants to work for a positive leader.

COMMUNICATING CULTURE

The other benefit of constantly giving awards against values is that you are reinforcing them time and time again. And never underestimate how many times you need to reinforce and communicate messages to teams. The first time you tell people, most will only hear what they want to hear. The second time they get a small amount of the message and then this can build over time. But you need to change the way you communicate to people; don't rely on the same way over and over. I used to hold "brown-bag" sessions with teams, which were discussions over a sandwich lunch asking how I could help the rest of the team, while all the senior team always used to take time at new-hire orientation meetings. Finally you should ensure that you have an open-door policy. When people want to see you or speak to you they are most likely to be receptive to whatever messages you want to get across to them.

WHAT'S IN AN OFFICE?

At LOVEFiLM I would say one of the most important factors in our cultural success was the office. Everything was completely open plan. We all sat together in the business, running the business. In fact, you could probably throw a single blanket (albeit king-size) and cover the desks of the chief financial officer, chief marketing officer, chief technology officer and myself (the chief executive). You may think that there is no privacy in this situation, but there were always other meeting rooms people could use if they needed to. And if we needed to make a decision, we would either stand up and chat about it, or pull up a small table and have a quick discussion. Then we could make a decision and move on. Speed of decision making is critical in any organization, but especially in a small, fast-growing one. You need to involve lots of people in the discussion so that you get the right answer, but you can't coordinate a two-hour long meeting, two weeks in the future, to agree what you are going to do. I passionately believe one area of strategic advantage for smaller companies is in speed of decision making. So make sure you protect this at all costs. Office layout makes a massive difference here. One of the reasons I believe Amazon has grown so quickly and continues to do so is because they have never lost that ability to make quick, well-informed and detailed decisions.

FINDING A COMMON ENEMY

It is really important in business to have a common enemy, somebody you are trying to beat. In the early days Video Island and LOVEFiLM (see Chapters 4 and 5) were constantly at each other. When we merged the two businesses, we had a few months of the "sleeping with the enemy" syndrome as covered in Chapter 6. This happened again in 2008, when we acquired Amazon's DVD rental customer base. Suddenly the company we were targeting was part of us.

In fact I think we lost some of our "edge" for a period of time after that. And we were only able to reignite it by focusing on Sky and Virgin, especially in the video on demand and online, streaming segments. In fairness, News Corp/Sky is a pretty easy company to line up against. I have never experienced a company that so many people dislike, as is evident in the press on a now daily basis.

But it is an awesome competitor business and I have the utmost respect for how it does things. Having set ourselves up against big boys we wanted to win that battle. After the launch of Netflix in the UK, I think even Sky realized that we were targeting them, as a lot of their advertising became focused on movie services and how many movies they had in the box. We had previously taken on Blockbuster Video and other DVD rental stores in the early days and won that battle, we had merged with similar companies to us and now we were kicking the 800lb gorilla. Now that is how you galvanize a culture.

CHAPTER 16

HOW TO SELECT AND MANAGE INVESTORS

Most of the people reading this book will know the difference between equity investment and debt investment and this is not meant to be a *Raising Money 101* or *Funding for Dummies*, as there are many better qualified people to write about these things than me. In fact, if there is such a book I am pretty sure I should read it. But I can share some experiences from LOVEFiLM that might be useful.

ENTER THE DRAGON'S DEN

Most people are aware of the BBC2 show *Dragon's Den* and its various spin-offs. In these TV shows innocent, would-be entrepreneurs present their ideas to a panel of seasoned pros and there is only ever going to be one outcome, cash wins out. This was also true at LOVE-FiLM. But the VCs we worked with were exceptionally professional, experienced and great fun (yes, that is fun) to work with.

In the early days, Video Island and ScreenSelect were competing in the DVD rental space. In my view ScreenSelect had better systems, a better brand and stronger management. But it was Video Island that bought the other company because, through its investors, it had more cash and could afford to. Sometimes it is not always the best idea or even the best execution that works. Cash is often king. This acquisition created a stronger combined business and it was at this stage that I joined.

FOUR'S COMPANY

As a result of this deal and the later merger with LOVEFiLM in 2006, we ended up with four VCs on the board. These were Index, Benchmark (now Balderton), Cazenove (now DFJ Esprit) and Arts Alliance Media. There were also other investor groups (Octopus and Redbus) who were not on the board. This meant we had lots of experience and help to call on. And they were a great help to the business and it all worked out well, on the whole.

But if I was starting again to look for funding, my advice would be to pick investors you best feel you can work with over the long term. It is not only about the amount of cash for equity you get. It is about how you work together and whether you think that when the going gets tough (and it inevitably will) you think you can fight it out together. Our VCs had different cultures and strengths, all of which came to the fore at different times. Some were better negotiators, some better networkers and some technically better in the industry. At all the different stages of business growth we actually needed to call on these different skills to help us.

A COMMON PURPOSE

In the early days it takes time to get aligned so that you have a shared vision of where the business is going and what you actually need to do. It is worthwhile taking that time, even if you thought you were aligned in the pitch process, to ascertain that you are still there, so that you have a good history of working together before the proverbial hits the fan. Opinions are like noses, everybody has one and they all smell. If you have lots of people around the table, you will have lots of opinions. You only earn respect by delivering. There is no other way to do this but give yourself as good a head start as you can.

"It is worthwhile taking time to ascertain that you are still aligned, so that you have a good history of working together before the proverbial hits the fan."

DIFFERENT TYPES OF INVESTMENT

The investment in Video Island in the early days was what is called preference shares. This is typical and normally means that when a company is sold, the VCs will get the cash out they invested first and then everything else will be paid out to shareholders on a percentage basis, including the VCs. You can say in order to invest their money they wanted to "double dip". This is a tried and trusted structure for VCs, but in my opinion it can lead to a number of problems. It meant management and the minority shareholders no longer wanted to raise money, because it was too expensive. In the early days of the business that meant that there was a resistance to raise money, and a natural limitation on how quickly it could grow.

Fortunately Simon Cook, one of our VCs, introduced us to the concept of venture debt. This is where you raise money secured against a working asset. In our case this was our DVD library. We raised cash for growth, but not at the expense of pure equity, especially preference "double dip" equity. This was a huge boost to the business and growth. We were able to remove the preference share structure at the time of the merger with LOVEFiLM and this made a huge difference in the alignment between management and the investors.

IF YOU NEED IT, CALL FOR HELP

After the merger between Video Island and LOVEFiLM in 2006, I called in expert help. I was spending a lot of time with investors in the first year and I needed to spend more time in the business after the merger. The board approved the hiring of Charles Gurassa as non-executive chairman. He was a fantastic help in managing all the different groups. Not only did he act as a confidante and mentor, he helped me by rolling up his sleeves at the right time when we needed to get into the detail with the different investor groups. The truth is that in any transaction, it is difficult to please everybody. Charles did a great job of steering us through some choppy waters.

LOOKING FOR THE EXIT

When you work with VCs, or any private equity investors, you need to know right at the start that there is going to have to be an exit at some stage. Their business model is based upon investing an amount of money and selling that investment for a larger amount. Not all of their deals achieve this, so the ones that do have to cover the ones that don't quite make it. Any successful venture will be under a pressure to sell. Therefore you need to plan and prepare for this exit as early as you can. And this doesn't mean selling up as early as you can. The learnings from LOVEFiLM on this are as follows:

1. Identify potential exit partners early on and make sure you build a relationship with them. Don't hold off speaking to a potential partner until you have reached a certain size. If they are a competitor, don't divulge facts. But most mergers and acquisitions happen because there is the right chemistry in the deal (i.e. the people like you) as much as because the financials stack up. I met the Amazon team in 2005. The deal wasn't done for another six years, by which time we knew each other very well. But the seeds were sown very early on. Of course I didn't only ask one girl to dance, but in the end most of us only get to take one girl home.

2. Constantly update your "elevator pitch" or speech. You will be asked at least a hundred times during any selling process to give a short, five-minute version of the reason why your company is worth anything. Make sure you can do this cold and understand the key "hot buttons" of people interested in the deal.

3. Collect your key "proof points" or bits of information for use in this pitch as you go along. If you find in customer research a single data point that supports your case, make sure you keep it with all the others. At LOVEFiLM we had about five or six killer facts we collected over the years. These undisputed facts made our story unique. This made all the difference. It is no different if you are still building a business plan. It is exactly the same process. You just will have to work with more assumptions and fewer facts.

4. When you are working with companies that are looking to buy you, think about the culture of their business and how it matches with yours. If there is any mismatch, the deal is less likely to happen. And don't underestimate what your company can bring to a larger, more established company. Often if you are quicker in decision making, have a unique technology or products, then you can also add a lot more to their business

than just revenues or profits (although hopefully you have some of those as well).

5. Be patient, but recognize the importance of timing. Don't force a deal or you will come over as desperate. But if the world is changing around you and new competitors are coming in to the industry, don't drag your heels.

6. Don't forget the staff. You need to bring them along with you, so spend time communicating with them and getting those communications right. They are an important part of any sale. It's true that the people are the most important assets of most businesses today and if they don't want to do it, the whole deal can unravel. At the time of the announcement, when you can go public, spend a lot of time with the staff. Both of the big deals we did at LOVEFiLM made sense. The merger with Video Island and LOVEFiLM helped us get critical mass. And the deal with Amazon got us the firepower to win in the long term. This made internal communications so much easier.

7. After the deal is done, don't forget it is now day one and not the last day. The new owners will have plans with lots of new opportunities. Keep something in your tank as you will need the energy in the new place to make it all happen and to deliver against the deal promises.

WHY AMAZON?

"Amazon has been able to keep hold of many of the factors and characteristics that drive success in smaller companies. This has given it a real advantage over other large companies."

Lots of people ask me this question. Disappointing it may be for some, but my answer only covers what is already public knowledge and has been quoted in the press. To compete in today's entertainment industry, against the likes of Sky and Google, you need a lot of firepower. Acquiring new content is getting more expensive. We looked at a number of different options for LOVEFiLM, including a public listing and private equity. But Amazon shared the same vision for the industry as LOVEFiLM. The difference was it had the money to invest to make it happen. The deal took a while to get done and I think it was our growing digital expertise, which Amazon felt it could use, that swung the deal. Since the acquisition, Amazon has lived up to its promise of investing in the business. Netflix has since launched in the UK and, to be honest, LOVEFiLM would not have been able to compete with it without the support of Amazon. It is unusual, but Amazon has been able to keep hold of many of the factors and characteristics that drive success in smaller companies. This has given it a real advantage over other large companies. And this is one of the reasons why it has been able to carry on growing. That is quite an achievement for a $40 bn turnover business.

CHAPTER 17
THE CLOSING CREDITS

There is a widely held and underlying common metaphor in much
of what we say and do in life that describes everything in terms
of a journey. This is especially true in business, where approaches
to areas such as strategy are framed in terms of starting points
and ideal destinations. But the truth is that, as with much of life, if
business is a journey, it is one undertaken if not blind then at
least with one eye closed. This was certainly the case with the LOVE-
FiLM story. When we set off, we certainly had no idea that the journey
ahead would be anywhere near as exciting, demanding or fulfilling as
it was. I hope I have been able to convey some of the thrill I experienced in playing a part in determining the eventual route our journey
took. But I also hope that there are lessons to be learnt from our
experiences.

Along the way we experienced a number of wild and well-celebrated
successes as well as having to deal with our fair share of shocks, fires
and failures. If my story has appeared to dwell more on successes than
failures, that is partly because I am an unashamed optimist and
someone who thinks in terms of challenges rather than problems, but
also because in the course of the relatively short time that I was at
LOVEFiLM, it was a phenomenally successful venture.

This success, and especially the rapid growth that underpinned that
success, would never have been possible without the people who were
around at the time. This includes the founders and key staff, the investors and the VCs many of whom have figured in this story. But not
everybody has a role all of the time and there is a time for everything.
The founders who launched the various businesses that eventually
merged to become LOVEFiLM, and the early key staff at those firms,
all played a vital role in getting the venture going and growing.
Although some had left or left soon after my involvement began, they
nevertheless planted many seeds that I was lucky enough to help
nurture into eventual successes.

But of course there were also many people who were strapped in
beside me, undertook that journey with me and importantly who

helped me ride the bumps along the way. A key part of the role of the leader in any organization is to bring those people with you. The strong focus on culture and the clearly defined values that we created at LOVEFiLM helped to make that part of the CEO's role easier, because it helped to make it a naturally exciting place to work. People wanted to be part of the LOVEFiLM story.

There is another well-used business saying that success breeds success. And it's true that once we had created the momentum with the huge "Braveheart" advertising campaign, finding future partners was certainly easier. Choosing the right partner in the end is absolutely critical to making the whole venture feel worthwhile

I know that as my career moves onto its next phase with Mothercare, I personally will be taking all sorts of learning and experience from my time at LOVEFiLM. I hope that I will be able to apply most of these lessons in my new role and well into my future career. I hope you find them useful as well.

If there is one overriding message I want people to take from this book, it is simply to go for it and seek to draw from every experience you possibly can. In any career and in any environment you can always draw something from the events and the experiences, the people and places around you.

Don't close down your options by only thinking about one type of organization. I started life working in a small shop, graduated to working at some of the world's largest organizations and then switched back to helping LOVEFiLM, then a small start-up, become one of the UK's most successful fast-growth businesses and ultimately part of one the largest companies in the world. I know therefore that there are lessons to be learnt from both big and small companies. If you follow your passion and are true to yourself, you can succeed in whatever you set out to do. You may not always know the direction of your journey, but if you make sure you enjoy the ride, that lack of knowledge won't ever hold you back.

PART ONE – PRE-PRODUCTION

CHAPTER 1 – OPEN ALL HOURS

1. **Don't underestimate the importance of understanding numbers** and getting to know the metrics behind a business when you are young.
2. **Get early experience of managing people.** I did that through things like the Athletic Union, being house captain, directing plays and captaining the rugby team.
3. **Learn to appreciate the importance of cash.** The most powerful lesson in business is the importance of cash. Its importance hasn't diminished one bit.
4. **Seek out some customer service experience early on** and learn all about what excellent customer service looks like. Working in the supermarket taught me about customer service and about the importance of milestones to help you get what you want to achieve.
5. **Understand the implications of everything you do.** I also managed my father's shop in the summer and I always wanted to beat his revenues and takings. I sometimes dented his gross margin percentage, but I beat his revenue target every time.
6. **If you don't innovate, competitors will steal customers.** My Dad's shops lost out to the major supermarkets. It's difficult to change when you are doing well, but doing it then is more effective. Leave it too late and you don't have time to get it right.
7. **Try as many different things as possible while you can.** Unless you are going to be really good at one thing, the more you expose yourself to new things the better. You never know where your strengths lie. And you will meet more interesting people along the way.

CHAPTER 2 – LEARNING THE MULTINATIONAL WAY

1. **Make sure work is fun.** As a leader, do whatever you can to make sure that people who work for you enjoy their work.

2. **Always look for simple solutions first.** If not everything can be fixed with a hammer, we can still overcomplicate problems.
3. **Understanding the numbers and metrics that are most important to measure** and knowing how you can effectively measure them is vitally important in any successful business.
4. **Make sure any new product or service benefits everyone involved.** Whether it's a new start-up or within a large organization, it has to offer benefits to all stakeholders.
5. **Know the data you need to run your business**, the ideal frequency you need it and how you will use it once you get it. And also how you can make sure you get the accuracy in it you need.
6. **Never reinvent something if what you need is already there.** Be prepared to borrow good stuff that already exists, as long as it's done legally.
7. **Take time to enjoy what you do and the experiences you are having.** It's essential that you relax as much as you can and enjoy things while they are happening.

CHAPTER 3 – BECOMING A DELL BOY

1. **Start with a structure and select the best people.** Don't start a new venture with structure made to fit the whims and preferences of people you like. You have to think equally about the best structure and the best people from the start.
2. **It is not enough just to employ brilliant people**, you need to employ them in a brilliant structure, and you need them to be doing the right stuff.
3. **The motivators for behaviour at work are universal.** Wherever people are based, and regardless of cultural context, they mostly want the same things.
4. **Strategy is simpler than people make out.** But when it comes to it, all you need to think about is what are you trying to achieve, how will you get there and that you are sure you are focused on the right activities to do that.

5. **Start-ups should aspire to the best big company thinking.** And in the same way, large corporates should aspire to be more entrepreneurial.

6. **Transparency is key to success.** A business can only be successful in the long term when there is total transparency within the organization about metrics. Everybody has to see everything. It's the best way to make everyone accountable.

7. **If cash is king, a positive cash conversion cycle is the power behind the throne.** A good business model means that every new customer brings in more revenue than they cost the business.

PART TWO – THE LOVEFiLM YEARS

CHAPTER 4   2003-4: THREE MEN AND A BABY

1. **Success has many fathers, while failure is an orphan.** It may be irritating, but be prepared to recognize that it often takes several people to make a business successful.

2. **A good idea is not enough.** There are plenty of good ideas that haven't worked. You also need a range of other factors and elements to come together.

3. **Put the right talent in the right roles.** And if you don't have that, you might have to go and find it, either by recruiting someone or merging with another business that has those skills.

4. **You need an aligned board behind you,** offering external advice and support, but all facing in the same way and not out for their own ends.

5. **Don't underestimate the importance of a strong balance sheet and plenty of cash.** Every business needs cash, especially in the early stages.

6. **Don't let the pursuit of excellence get in the way of good.** While it is important to take time to get things right at the start, don't let it stop you from getting things moving. You can improve as you grow.

7. **Always be prepared to meet people,** both new people and existing contacts, because you never know where those meetings will lead.

CHAPTER 5 *2005: TOWERING INFERNO*

1. **Never underestimate your strength in a crisis.** It can be surprising how strong you and the people around you can be when something terrible happens.
2. **Prepare all you can for the worst-case scenario.** Too often, being prepared for possible crises is seen as a luxury limited to larger companies. It should be a necessity for all organizations.
3. **Have a 100-day plan from the start.** When you join a new organization, especially in the top job, have a clear 100-day plan and stick to it. It allows you to set out what you want to do and establish a framework for your style.
4. **Have a positive cash conversion.** The real secret to achieving fast growth is to have a positive cash conversion cycle.
5. **Negotiate from strength when you can.** Speak to banks, lenders and other suppliers when things are going well. Don't wait until you need them to start those conversations.
6. **Keep control of your own destiny.** Do what you can to make sure the destiny of your business is in your own hands, even if that means taking radical action.
7. **Speak to senior industry people as often as possible.** If you want to get insight and intelligence, go directly and speak to the most senior people you can. Always ask them at the end of any meeting who else you should speak too.

CHAPTER 6 *2006: SLEEPING WITH THE ENEMY*

1. **Good leaders spot their own mistakes quickly**, admit to them, adjust their thinking, make any required changes and move on.
2. **Keep your eye on your customers at all times**, but especially at times of change. It may sound trite, but change often makes people focus internally and lose sight of their customers.
3. **During times of change, focus your attention on the employees staying.** Any restructuring means you will lose people, and too much attention goes to those who leave. Don't forget those staying behind. They are the future so focus on them.

4. **Appoint someone independent to lead your board.** An external view and balance can make all the difference when times get tough.
5. **An organization's values should come from within**, not from external consultants. Employees know what's important to them and what's not, so sit down with them and hold meetings and talk about what matters and pull out themes.
6. **Don't shy away from or outsource difficult conversations.** It's important to get involved and do handle them yourself.
7. **Take time to get your share structure right.** It is vital in getting everyone aligned, from the management to the board to the external investors.

CHAPTER 7   2007: BRAVEHEART

1. **Sometimes you have to bet big**, in order to win anything worthwhile.
2. **Controlled risk taking is good for business, reckless gambles are not.** A positive attitude to risk doesn't mean you can't do all you can to reduce the chance of failure.
3. **It's impossible to overstate the importance of brand awareness for consumer brands.** Always spend as much as you can afford on targeted marketing that raises your brand profile but be ready for it if it takes off.
4. **There are more ways to fund a business than you imagine.** Look at other ways to fund business growth than simple bank lending or giving away equity.
5. **Make the effort to understand difficult people.** Getting rid of star performers can be an expensive mistake. Stars can be difficult to manage, but sometimes it's worth the effort if they can stay true to your behaviours and values.
6. **Have the courage to act quickly to get rid of people who aren't performing.** The sooner it's done, the better for all parties.
7. **Your teams will learn it is OK to fail if you admit your own mistakes.** Be brave and put your hands up when you get it

wrong, they will support you even more and take more risks themselves.

CHAPTER 8 2008: THE GODFATHER

1. **Leaders must be firm as well as fair.** While effective leaders need to be aware of the softer people skills and be emotionally engaged, it's also important to be seen to be decisive and to act quickly.
2. **Be wary of big businesses expressing an interest in buying some or all of your business.** They won't value your time as much as you do and they often turn out to be wasting time.
3. **Listen to all serious offers, and be polite but resolute. Do what you can to learn about them.** Discovering how you fit with their plans may help your strategy.
4. **Make sure you are in the room with the right people.** Don't settle for anyone less than the key decision maker.
5. **Keep all conversations open and moving.** It's very difficult to predict which ones will pay off and which ones will go nowhere.
6. **Don't forget to prepare for life after the deal.** While sealing a big deal is exciting and motivating, make sure you work to integrate organizations fully.
7. **Don't think customers care about things just because you do.** What matters in terms of organizational structure, for example, isn't of interest to customers.

CHAPTER 9 2009: GROUNDHOG DAY

1. **Growth can be a grind.** While the early years in business are about excitement and change, to achieve lasting growth you need to get down to the grind of day-to-day business. It can seem boring, but the hard slog is worth it in the end.
2. **Fast growth means growing up.** There comes a tipping point when you move from being a collection of passionate people just

muddling through, to being an organization with structure and order. You have to act to create that structure.

3. **Not all entrepreneurs are good at running a mature business.** You may need a different leadership team as the business grows up. Keep the founder involved as long as it makes sense but make sure everyone knows the strengths and weaknesses they bring to the table.

4. **You never get everything right first time, but you must ensure you do stuff and constantly change.** Be on the lookout for when things are wrong and be prepared to change course. Constantly adapt to get to perfection rather than wait for it before doing anything, but be prepared to have to work to achieve it.

5. **Allow and encourage managers to manage.** Insist on instigating a decent performance management process, it will allow your managers to understand what is happening in their teams and help them make decisions accordingly. Publically recognize the high performers, make them feel special.

6. **Set big, audacious goals and let all staff know what they are.** Then make sure you celebrate and reward everyone when you achieve them.

7. **Data can be addictive and can paralyze you.** Don't let the wait for perfect data stifle growth or innovation. But set out knowing the key metrics and information you need to run the business well and grow it quickly.

CHAPTER 10   2010: SLEEPLESS IN SEATTLE

1. **Business is unpredictable.** Don't try to prejudge the outcome of a situation in business. Especially in a fast-growth business and a dynamic industry, almost anything can happen.

2. **Keep your options open.** Because anything might happen you never know which meetings might turn out to be significant. Don't turn down an opportunity to meet someone interesting, because something interesting might come from it.

3. **All deals take longer than you expect.** You need patience in negotiation. No matter how simple a deal looks, there are always

complicating factors to overcome. It will take longer than you thought it would. And it will cost more.

4. **Always negotiate for a win/win.** Trying to score points over someone else usually ends in disaster. Work hard for an outcome that pleases everyone a bit.

5. **Don't let big personalities spoil a deal.** Insist on instigating a decent performance management process, it will allow your managers to understand what is happening in their teams and help them make decisions accordingly.

6. **Pick your advisors and non-executives carefully.** During the run-up to the sale we hired some great non-execs that helped when it came to the sale. We trusted them fully at all times to do what was right for us. As you've spent time and money hiring them, then listen carefully to their advice when they offer it.

7. **Predicting technology can be tough.** Be prepared to get it wrong. Don't stubbornly stick to a path if the industry data and intelligence suggest you are wrong.

CHAPTER 11   2011: JERRY MAGUIRE

1. **A difficult deal can take over your life.** But if you want the best outcome for a short time you might have to let it. The rewards will be there in the end.

2. **Don't expect everyone to see the deal the way you do.** The staff response to the Amazon deal was overwhelmingly positive, but some observers were critical of what they saw as a "sell-out".

3. **Start with the end in mind.** Make sure you understand what a win looks like for both parties before you start negotiating and make sure your entire board is aligned behind what you think is a win.

4. **Understand what investors want at the start.** It is likely that they will want to have a seat on the board and a say in the future running of the business. Don't enter negotiations if you won't settle for that.

5. **Opinions are like noses.** Everyone has one and all of them are different. And some don't smell as good as others. Respect everyone's view, but only if they are being reasonable.
6. **Be prepared for change.** Doing a big deal with a major investor will inevitably change the culture of your own organization. Don't expect to act like a small company when you are part of a much larger one.
7. **Plan your succession early.** Right from the start when hiring my executive team I thought about who could and would take over if something happened to me.

ABOUT THE AUTHOR

Simon Calver was CEO of LOVEFiLM, the online DVD and Digital Entertainment company from 2005 to 2012 when it was sold to Amazon Inc.

He previously worked with Unilever in brand, marketing and key account roles and PepsiCo where he was Vice President in charge of the UK business launching Pepsi Max, Pepsi Blue and the development of the Pepsi Music activity. With PepsiCo he was also VP Sales Operations managing worldwide franchise partners and best practise selling and operational skills globally, specialising in developing and emerging markets.

After Pepsi he was GM and VP for Dell Home and Small Business operations based in Ireland and also COO and President of Riverdeep Inc., the interactive digital education company where he led the turnaround after a management buyout.

In April 2012 he became Chief Executive of Mothercare plc the global Mother and Baby retailer.

He has led businesses in London, New York, Dublin, San Francisco and currently lives in West London with Cathy and their son Monty and their new arrival Nieve.

ACKNOWLEDGEMENTS

It is often quoted that success has many fathers, while failure is an orphan. Well LOVEFiLM certainly had its fair share of fathers and deservedly so. The business would never have been the success it was without a class team to lead it.

In the book I cover many of the founders involved in the early days of the business, but the management from Fern, Lesley, both Simons, Mike, Andrew, David and Jim were the best I have seen. The fun, challenges and camaraderie we had on this roller-coaster ride were highlights of my career so far. Their infectious enthusiasm and perhaps the partial insanity, especially Simon Morris, helped keep my feet firmly on the ground. I miss you all.

Investors and venture capitalists are often maligned in the current economic climate, but I can't fault those involved at LOVEFiLM. They all had passion, drive and importantly contacts, that we selfishly used at every opportunity. In particular Danny Rimer at Index, George Coelho at the then Benchmark, Simon Cook at DFJ Esprit and the irrepressible Thomas Hoegh of Arts Alliance Media all played a role, often at different times, supporting me and the business.

I also had great support from the chair, initially from Simon Murdoch and then for over five years from Charles Gurassa, whose wise counsel helped us in many and varied situations. We would not have done the deal without him. Thank you also to David Carter for helping me step out of my shadow during the whole process. And I would like to thank Bill Carr and Greg Greeley from Amazon for their vision in how LOVEFiLM and Amazon could work together and I wish them the best of luck with all of their endeavours with the business.

While pulling together this book one very real challenge was to separate the useful from the not relevant, despite being so close to the events. I can't claim credit for achieving this, as it was through many sessions and late nights that the writing and editing craft of Richard Cree came to the fore. He was able to capture not only the passion in my experiences but put it down in words that resonated for me. It was through the repeated drafting and survival through crashed hard-drives and computer thefts that we got to know each other very well. I look forward to our next venture together.

I would like to thank Holly Bennion at Wiley for sticking with me during all of the job changes that went on. Her enthusiasm and drive for the project kept me to the ever-slipping deadlines. Her team of Jenny Ng, Sam Hartley and Vicky Kinsman have helped make this happen and I thank them all.

Finally I would like to thank Cathy, not only for being the best cheerleader, chief editor and all the support I could wish for, but along with Monty and Nieve, for giving real meaning to the importance of a good work-life balance.

INDEX

Index compiled by Annette Musker